'EIGHT MONTHS IN LECCE'
by Carol Fors

CHAPTER ONE – OCTOB

OCTOBER 2nd

Three exhausting flights are akin to giving birth; an ordeal but worthwhile in the end. Arriving at Brindisi airport this afternoon was surprisingly relaxing: A small compact hub without any fuss or bother. Scooping up my ample cases and piling into a taxi, the driver alluded to the fact that town loyalties are strong. My inquisitive questions about Lecce, down in the heel of Italy's Salento, were met with some reserve, but I could tell, reading between the lines, that it was a place of great beauty, and one to be absorbed at a leisurely pace, were it ever possible.

The car journey saw olive groves and small deserted palazzi; a palm tree here or there under still warm October skies. What struck me the most on this journey, was how the modern motorway with its racing cars contrasted with such quiet beauty on its flanks. Ancient and modern, hand in hand.

My first views of the city were confused yet optimistic - some Roman remains here, a dirty billboard there, all in hues of pastel. The sun overhead, created the sense of entering a frame, perhaps a bit claustrophobic, but nonetheless positive. Sunny streets stretched on with elegant golden bathed palazzi swathed with their lush gardens and Baroque features. Baroque is the next big thing that affects. Baroque everywhere. Intricate, delicate Baroque. An aesthetic delight. A sense of sleepiness pervades. Sleepy but all in hand, if that makes sense. Strolling people, nothing fast. The taxi arrived at my hotel. A modern affair, with the usual Italian flair for decor and architecture. Marbled floors lay cool in the afternoon sun and a friendly dog yapped on the street. Ushered into the cooling vibes and led up to

my room, womb-like dark corridors led me in. My first reaction once inside was quiet relief. I'd travelled from Manchester to Brindisi, without incident and arrived safely at my destination.

Ordering a caffeine-fuelled cappuccino only served to show how exhaustion is. I woke up hours later...

OCTOBER 5th

Several days in and I'm beginning to understand how it works here. I'm even beginning to know where I am and how to get where I'm heading. Perched on the fifth floor of an apartment block, my neighbours are a mixture of reserve and curiosity. I've been asked at least five times why I don't use the lift. I don't like lifts – even aesthetically pleasing Italian ones. The emergency button clearly hasn't been used recently and I don't imagine anyone rushing to the enfeebled buzzer if it was.

I stick to my guns and avoid it like the plague, to the consternation of some fellow house dwellers. The old lady below pokes her head out from time to time, like an ancient tortoise, with great suspicion and an eye for the comings and goings. A friendly wave doesn't really change things but these things take time. My flat is a cosy place and always warm.

The heat rises continually, so I wander around without the cardigan.

My room is large, very large indeed, like a cathedral with acoustics that reverberate constantly.

I can hear the neighbours. I hear them shouting, laughing, singing, fighting. I can hear the street - the crazy guy that shouts to no one; the trumpet player; the shopkeepers and friends. I can hear the dogs barking a reply and the naughty bambino whose mother scolds him. I hear the whoosh whoosh of the washing machine and the hoover. I have fifty students to teach so I buy ear plugs and bless them each and every day. Then one day, the drilling starts ...

OCTOBER 7th

Living five floors up has its moments. Sometimes I wake up to eerie sounds that are not of this world; peculiar ones I can't quite place. I sometimes hear the treading of floorboards from above, yet I'm told the flat's been empty for years since the old girl died. Sometimes it's the clinking of glass or the sharp shutting of a door. At those times I retreat a little further under my duvet and try to fall back to sleep so I'm here, all lonesome, with the spooks.

When dawn arrives, the light seeps through the slats and sends straight digits across my room. The rattly roller lifts the blinds to reveal a generous balcony above the shop-lined street below.

I meander along towards the old centre. It's a smart and organized affair with all in its place.

When I reach the main parts, I take a small side street near the upmarket hotel by Via Umberto and find several tiny back street shops. Entering one, the goods are placed neatly in fridges and on shelves: A melon here, some cheese there. Iced water snugs by milk near the pasta shelf. The old man yawns on his chair and reads the paper. A mugshot on the front reminds me that perfection doesn't exist, yet this simple shop is probably just as it was some fifty years before and makes me wonder.

I walk along to Sant'Oronzo and stand by the Roman amphitheatre. Beside sits a toothless man and nearby some African street vendors, leaning by a wall. Looking down into the Roman ruins, I spot a lizard frozen on a wall. A cat wanders by then jumps gracefully from ancient stone to the square.

The sun is low but a gentle warmth soothes the scene.

Bars take care of the early birds and a thousand stories begin to unfold for the day.

Walking across I reach a quiet place to sit and contemplate. Still trying to acclimatize, I'm not yet sure how I feel about Lecce.

It has its positives, for sure.

Sometimes it strikes me where I am. I picture the boot of Italy and its heel. So here I am. I've never been so south before, apart from nearby Greece, but this isn't quite as you'd think.

Strolling a while along Via Vittorio Emanuelle, I spot the entrance to an arty place with second-hand stalls sprinkled with trinkets, old watches and cups sitting beside art work; the odd rug or throw.

Quite fascinated, I wander from stall to stall, and my eye is drawn to an old postcard of Lecce. It's black and white and on the back some old ink writes of simple things, like temperate weather and a trip to Gallipoli. The final sentence, grabs me: 'I didn't know that such a place exists'.

The general tone suggests positives yet that sentence is pregnant with meaning. I begin to wonder about the writer and what they were referring to. The old door behind me creaks open and more wares are brought through.

'I didn't know that such a place exists'. It's dated pre-war and the writing fades here and there, but those words are clear enough.

Wandering on through the town I enter a large bookshop. I'm always impressed by them here in Italy. The smell of unopened pages and unseen prose bewitches me a little and I don't leave empty handed. Buying a copy of Montale's poetry I sit awhile in a garden reading them.

As I walk back along the streets towards Piazza Mazzini, I think about the postcard again and wonder if the tourist was simply referring to the Baroque or was there other? I'll never know.

OCTOBER 9th

I now know the launderette, the newspaper shop, the greengrocer's and the luxury take-away. I now know my students. On Saturdays I walk to the town centre. This is not like your normal one but a small portion of splendour. Piazza Sant'Oronzo leads down Via Umberto where I stroll past the Basilica di Santa Croce, with its incredible Baroque facade, now encased in scaffolding, towards my favourite Saturday morning cafe. The Basilica is a treat for the curious, with bas-reliefs of artist Francesco Antonio Zimbalo of San Francesco di Paola's life. The golden light bathes everything. The beauty. The Baroque.

The quaint little shops. The ancient city walls. The classy Art galleries. All. Beauty. Piazza del Duomo is my second place. Here you find the 17th century Palazzo Vescovile and the Seminario adding balance to the majestical cathedral facing a spacious piazza near the cosy cafe with friendly waitress . So, as you sit in the October warmth of a snug den you can see all this magnificence before you, yet to explore.

OCTOBER 10th

It's 3 am and I can't sleep. The couple below are arguing animatedly, and the gurgling water tank is doing its thing. I have a lot of lessons today, so I am not amused and start to muse on the best ways to fall back asleep. In the end I decide to re-read the section on phrasal verbs in my TEFL book which does the trick. Starting to yawn, it works but only to be wakened again at six by some friendly banter outside and someone closing an apartment door. I bounce into action, as I find this the best way to get up of a morning. No slow sleepy approach, but a full on activation strategy. Skipping down the five flights of stairs and narrowly avoiding my inquisitor, regarding my predilection for stairs over lifts, I emerge into a sunlight infused street and head for the corner cafe. Here are the glamorous people; the well dressed and no doubt well-heeled members of the community. The owner looks stressed as usual but decides to try out his English on me. 'You are English?' he shares with those present, who grin in much the way you would grin at a monkey's antics at the zoo. I play along and congratulate his English, which is only fair and seem to get an exalted cappuccino this morning which arrives promptly, to the consternation of an impatient regular, all froth to perfection.

A yappy little dog looks at me preciously, as if wanting the same attentions. It's clinging for dear life to its pet. Its pet is wearing an Armani suit with all the most up-to-date trimmings. He is suitably attired for Lecce and Lecce is suitably attired for him. His aftershave fills the room and so does he. My fat, squelchy Cornetto slips onto the table into a jammy splurge. Oh the horror!

Che brutta figura!

I might go to the more down-to-earth bar next time. Today I have my class of small bambini. These pre-school children take some getting used to. They are as smart as I phones and twice as with it. Little Mario has reminded me of my place, 'Why are you talking in this

stupid language to me?' It's hard to know if this is meant in an existential sense or not! It brings a smile to my day but it's a tough question to answer to a four year old who just wants

to play with the orange truck.

OCTOBER 11th

Looking down at broken paving stones on the way to school, I wonder if a sink-hole will appear and take me down into the bowels of Lecce. A sobering thought, I hurry and make each step matter, like some expert mountaineer. Strange shops to my right are busy in the day's endeavours and the odd Vespa pulls up to a garage.

I decide to spend a while in the bar opposite my school to fuel up for the morning's work and find a large empty seat. Beside are several newspapers and I plump for 'La Gazzetta del Mezzogiorno'. The news, the usual mix of good and bad with photos of this accident or incident or incomer, all there emblazoned on each fresh page.

The bar is well organized and orange spremutas performed on request. As each sweet citrus fruit is fed into the machine, a satisfying notch up the thirst ensues and so I sit quietly with my drink and paper, preparing for my day.

To the right, some old men sit chatting loudly of this injustice or that. They're opinionated yet their bonds of friendship clear.

Then, as I go to pay, I sense a presence next to me.

'Buongiorno Signora', says he. He enquires if I am one of the new English teachers, clearly knowing the answer already.

'Si' I reply.

Then he must be allowed to pay for my drinks and the morning's Cornetto yield, says he.

'Benvenuto. Sono Ernesto. And you are?'

'Carol', I reply.

A little embarrassed I accept this gesture of friendship and thank the old man. And so I think, looking at him, that he's perhaps 80 and retired. Small, with thin grey hair, yet smartly dressed, he presents a picture of old Italy and I think no more of it, other than its warmth.

Time for school, I say goodbye and leave the bar into the sunny street, but then I notice a presence again. It's Ernesto. Behind him his old friends give gestures of approval and grins.

'Let me accompany you to the door, Signora'.

You realise this is about five paces, if that. Unclear how to react, the old man walks beside me, stopping the odd car with his walking stick. On reaching the door he says, 'It has been a pleasure to meet you, lovely Carol'. Feeling a little uncomfortable, I take my leave and hotfoot up the stairs. Almost expecting the old guy to follow, instead I see him return to the bar, to the applause of his friends. I guess it gives him something to do!

I nearly forget after lessons, but thankfully remember to look out for him, just in case he feels it his duty to accompany me home.

No sign of him, I hurry to the supermarket and buy a lunch of Tuna and Italian bread, a few plump olives to complete. Munching in the old Italian kitchen, I take in all the utensils: Small pans for boiling; tiny Espresso cups and strange spoons for pasta.

I hear people returning for lunch in adjacent flats and look out from a windowed balcony. A long way down, I see small children with their mamma and a tired dog on a lead; an old couple and some workmen.

Tired, I repair to my room and fall fast asleep. The jangly alarm on my phone sees me rushing to afternoon lessons. I take a slightly different route today as not in the mood for admirers. It takes me across the six-laned road, past residential apartment blocks and a row of shops. A travel agent sits squarely on the corner. Holidays to England! It strikes me bizarre, yet why not. Past the superior take-away I go, then the cheesemakers in their hats with great vats of the stuff, and the logo of the school.

Ernesto is nowhere to be seen. A gaggle of students arrive and so my day begins in earnest.

OCTOBER 12th

A man was shot today. Dead I believe. Somewhere in the suburbs. It doesn't really go with the perfection of a 75 degree day and the giggles of the children in the street. Shot dead? What affrontery. On a lighter note, I've heard the funny tale of one famous inhabitant throwing water on a rowdy scene below his balcony. Too noisy for him. City centre antics.

The evenings are lively here, as always in the cities and the towns. As anywhere. Even too much alcohol consumed. How sad, I think. It was one of my favourite things about Italy, the lack of a drinking culture, apart the civilized lunchtime vino.. It seemed a northern disease,. And yet the world is shrinking.

The shot man was in his 40s. I know not why. He'd just stepped out of his car for lunch and then they got him. Several shots straight for the heart. They didn't think much of his children's hearts or that of his wife. Widowed at 30.

The tourist is oblivious, taking shots of this and that, but not that sort. Like a parallel universe, they don't even see. Maybe if they care to read the paper, but most don't.

As I wander along Viale Japigia, past the zoo that is a garden, I look around at the gap-toothed one who staggers near the tobacconist's.

He's unwell in more ways than one. I see the mothers hurry children to the car or the Vespas scurry mindlesslly along. All very normal and routine. The President's porter stands outside chatting to the bar manager next door and they laugh at some humorous tale. All seems perfectly fine.

And so I think of a bowl of fruit, all plump and ripened, yet there in the middle might lurk the odd rotten one; even a few.

OCTOBER 14th

I have accepted the drilling as my lot and wake to the sound of the trumpet player whose parps drift around the palazzo, and no doubt all other buildings nearby. It's an upbeat way to start the day and as I look from my balcony, I see the merry street vendor outside the greengrocer shop, smiling amiably at passersby. I can't believe how quickly I've adapted to the place. Even the birds seem at home on my balcony, as if I had lived here a thousand years. My flatmates have arrived and moved into their rooms. One restores art, the other a student. Both simpatica, we go with the flow. Exquisite Italian meals begin to appear in the kitchen, and I observe with fascination how they are made. It's very warm today and I emerge into the world like a butterfly shedding its chrysalis. A golden light bathes the buildings and hugs all it graces. The nearby cafe is lively with early morning coffee drinkers, chatting and exchanging their views of the world. A small dog yaps excitedly at its ambivalent owner. The pet is perfectly presented with a beautiful red collar, but the owner doesn't seem to show much affection for the sad beast. Bella figura. The superficial is important here. A glamorous woman enters the cafe, wearing up to date fashion, every

seam in place. With an arrogant air, she orders her morning cappuccino, and is intolerant at its tardy arrival. The old man who runs the bar is exasperated with beads of sweat on his forehead. He distractedly gives the wrong drinks out, then barks at the waiter. The loud conversations drown out this mini drama and life resumes. It's 9 oclock and I head for the school, across the six-laned road, with life firmly in hands, past the strange shop with the wares for sale unclear; the perfumery and the post office, where disgruntled people queue at the cashpoint, then on to the stationers where all colours of paper and pen are on show. Here I peruse for a few items, marvelling at the array on offer yet wondering at their price. A sad street beggar enters the shop, looking anxious. He can't be more than 20. After a while he wanders out again, but it casts a sad shadow on the day.

On I walk, past Aqua e Sapone, the wonder toiletry store and the mini supermarket. I wave to the ladies at the old launderette as I pass, and the woman who works in the coffee shop then stop to stare at the fish shop window, with all its fishy glory and so

many species that I'm unfamiliar with, all as fresh as a dewdrop, there near the school.

Then finally, my pre school stop -the bar opposite. The smiling waitress and jolly

workers chat merrily before their day and I order a Fruits of the Forest filled Cornetto

with my cappuccino and watch it squelch onto my hands. The sticky gloop brings a

blush to my cheek, but it also brings a smile to my stomach.

Oh happy days!

OCTOBER 15th

Oh Lord please make the drilling stop! The heavy thuds of a hammer can also be heard as a

delightful adjunct to the early morning rise. Out of tea, I leave the flat in despair, and

walk briskly, zig-zagging the negotiable roads, to nearby Supermarket Dok. I have

decided that I'll succumb to any I can find, even the grey sock variety. With fevered

brow, I search for the drinks section. There, on the first aisle, not far from the entrance I

spot a small red box with the words 'English Breakfast Tea' written clearly upon it. It

has an authentic tea vibe to it, that pleases me, so I bypass the lesser varieties and pop it

optimistically into my trolley. Also into the trolley go Stracchino, bread, milk and water,

but it's the tea that sits there prettily, like a beautiful Christmas gift, waiting to be opened.

I hurry back to my apartment to enjoy said delicacy, and quickly put on some hot water in

a battered old pan. It seems to take forever to boil, but eventually does and so comes the

moment I've been waiting for. The moment of the morning. The grand christening of

the red-boxed tea bag. I swish and I swirl with a metal spoon and wait for the colour to

turn a mid tan, but it stubbornly refuses and stays a pale fawn hue. I press and I prod with the dear hope that something will miraculously change, but the colour remains. Taking a sip, it is almost pleasant, to my surprise, so I begin to contemplate the idea of a two tea bagged tea. The water a-boiling again, hubbling and bubbling with my rising anticipation at the outcome. The pair sit neatly side by side in the cup, awaiting their turn. In it goes, the hot water and a small dash of milk to complete the process. I watch eagerly as a child, waiting to see what colour this time. To my joy and relief, a nice suitably tea tan colour develops and I take an enthusiastic sip. Perfect. I'm happy. Two small red boxed tea bags equals one Tetley's tea bag. Well that's ok. Shame there are only five in the box. There has to be another way ...

OCTOBER 18th

Waking up early to start my day, I negotiate the snickets and alleyways near my apartment to reach the bigger shops. A lemon glow graces the modern buildings and palazzi, as the day unfolds. I've only been here a short while but sometimes feel a sense of being framed in concrete. A sea of shops and flats sit stubbornly through the quarter with traffic its companion.

Tomorrow, I will go somewhere else. I'd like to be with horizons of blue. It comes to me.

Trani.

I was there a few years ago. The gentle warmth saw us at a cafe, my husband and I, by the fishermen's catch whilst others mended nets. We'd gone with our Barlettan friend Rafaelle.

The marina bobbed before us and the quiet morning led us to the cream-stoned cathedral. I'll go there for sure.

The day's still early as I do my rounds, collecting this and that at the stationer's and fruit from the green grocer's. A gilding light guides my way and shopkeepers greet me as a newly arrived familiar. I also buy postcards to send home and stamps from the tobacconists, all neatly squared in a booklet, like the old green shield ones of yesteryear. Passing the launderette, a man appears as if from nowhere on his moped, up a small driveway from his apartment block. He skilfully weaves the cars and vans at quite a pace. Then, I work my way to Acqua e Sapone to buy things for the flat. A big swathe of coloured bottles baffles me awhile as I take in their content and purpose. Hovering then noticing the time, I pay and scurry back with all the goods.

On entering the palazzo, I see a smart old lady there before me

'Buongiorno, Signora' I say

'Buongiorno!' She frostily replies.

Enquiring who I am and why I'm here, she is enlightened as to my purpose and tells me, as if appointing herself Queen of Puglia, 'And I am Signora Rizzi.'

She then points to the lift and tells me to press the button. Catching me off guard, I break my rule to never use them, and like a lamb, climb in with my shopping.

'Brava!' She concludes.

And then, with neither smile nor frown, she watches until the ancient metal box does its thing. Arriving at the fifth floor to an uncomfortable clunk and delay in the opening of the creaky old metallic door, I am relieved to reach my own. Although laden, I'm even more resolved never to use the thing again.

Heavy banging outside would put paid to people hearing if you were stuck. That, and the fact they're all old and half deaf here.

Leaving my stuff, I rush down the five flights for the school. On arriving at the giant portone, Signora Rizzi casts a disapproving eye. Why, she enquires, didn't I use the lift on the way down?

I speedily reply some nonsense then make good my escape all school bound, past the posh patisserie and the bank and the set back apartments on the left.

I arrive five minutes early for morning class. Only four pupils, but bright and keen. We stumble our way through Simple Requests before lunch then I rush through chattering crowds and dawdlers to the six-laned road and wait eons to cross.

The satisfying clunk of my portone sees no Queen Bee and so, with stealth, I climb the stairs, quite guiltily, as if it were a crime. I hear the grumblings of a male voice on the 4th then reach the 5th. The old lady next door opens hers and stares with curiosity.

Unlike La Rizzi, she is reserved and simply greets me.

My lunch, the remnants of last night's pasta with a small square of Pecorino and a large apple for dessert.

Lying on my bed, I watch the fingers of lights through my old blind. It casts a glow over my throw and the marbled floor. The sweet smell of Lavender puts me into soft reveries and I fall asleep dreaming of Trani and the next day.

OCTOBER 19th

Trani.

The place is significant for me. Once an important, thriving port, it now sits in gentle sunbathed light by the sea. More sleepy, yet still vibrant. I travel on 'La Freccia Bianca' from Lecce. It takes a while up the Adriatic coast, watching pink-toned towns whizz by and the olive groves in sharp relief. Then arrival. I first came here in '89 working as a teacher in Barletta. Stayed some seven months or so. What a seven months! January. It was cold and the limestone paving stones a little icy.

I recall my breath in the winter air.

Creamy shades. Beauty. The cathedral, all limestone wedding cake. Three tiers from old to ancient furthest down. I stay overnight in a B&B complete with friendly dog, which wags so copiously every time it sees me, I begin to think that I exude some special aura.

The cafe by the waters give a view of fishermen mending nets and cyclists on their way to work by the sea, as alluring as ever, with boats completing the artist's dream.

I visit the cathedral once again, awestruck by the sheer beauty, there by the water; an ancient mustiness to the walls. And then in the evening I eat in the old restaurant by the marina. Simple sea food. Delicious. Then satiated, returned to the B & B, perhaps a fleeting visit, but enough just to take in the sea air and feel the space around me of a thousand years and some.

The ancient bustling port of old.

Enough to feel the seductive sea swooshing below and walk the wide paved stones.

It was hard to tear myself away from this beautiful place, but work was calling, so with a heavy heart, I boarded my Sunday train and returned to Lecce, past the olive groves and the graffitied posters; the autumn palms and the distant seascapes.

My return to Lecce saw me lesson planning in earnest and looking at my meagre cupboard to concoct a meal. I had pasta; a jar of olives; some garlic and olive oil. I also found a tin of Dok tomatoes so with a flourish prepared a delicious pasta meal and sat with a pen in one hand; a fork in the other.

The doorbell rang which set my nerves a jangling, but it was just the landlord delivering mail for me.

He darted here and there, without much in the way of words, then disappeared as quickly as he came, back down the rattly lift, past the shouty neighbours and down to the street where I could hear him being greeted by someone he knew.

A savage wind threw my shutter open and knocked my papers flying, so on closing it I restored the balance and equilibrium I'd lost and continued my work.

After a shower and some time on the phone reconnecting to my world, I fell fast asleep in preparation for the week ahead.

I was right all along.

The lift doesn't work and noone's been round to fix it. I also observed a tourist being ripped off at a local launderette today when his paltry bag of washing was charged an extortionate fifty Euros. He had the good sense to reject the offer and is probably, as we speak, grim-facedly trying to wash it in his hotel sink. Drying is no problem however and the thrill of hanging it out to see this miracle occur is worth the effort. I met a Canadian woman today at one of my favourite cafes. We sat awhile and chatted about Italy past and present both with that disquiet about our time here and both having lived here long ago.

Modern Italy does lack something.

Something has died, along with the internet. It's really sad, rather like trying to revive a long dead romance. To my horror, the bath plug fell right down the hole ...

OCTOBER 21ˢᵗ

My boss is multi talented – and male! He has successfully managed to fish out the offending plug from the deep dark depths of the plug-hole and now I can enjoy the unusual experience of a bath in Italy.

For some naive reason, I never imagined I would have baths in Italy and always had the shower in mind. Perhaps for that reason, the plunging of the plug seemed appropriate, as if baths were taboo here.

My students are great. I like them already and that's saying something as I'm not used to such amenable people, having worked in the English state school system for too long

Out onto the sunny streets of Lecce again, sunglasses propped neatly on my head, I am for my afternoon constitutional and obligatory cappuccino fix.

However, I'd quite forgotten to pick up my clothes from the laundry ladies near my school. Entering their place is like a trip back to the 1950s. Sublime. Old machinery does its stuff with the peaceful whirring and a wild whoosing; chemical odours fill the shop and the foreheads of workers perspire in the deadening heat, but they never complain, and are always to be found in the bar near my school at 3pm.

They sit as patiently as wise old owls, consuming their Espressos as fuel for the next shift. And so forth to my lessons at 3.55pm precisely. Such precision is futile as noone's arrived yet.

OCTOBER 22nd

I like Tuesdays as I have such fun in those classes. It's sometimes hard to be funny after five hours straight teaching so I remind myself that I am here as teacher, not comedienne. I am beginning to think I'm on the stage of 'London at the Palladium' or something, as entertainment abounds. My rusty Italian is improving now and sometimes, dare I say it, it is more of a language exchange, with my students gently correcting me and me the same. I'm looking forward to a large bowl of Penne all'Arrabbiata. This has been my favourite Italian meal for many years. There's just something about it - the fiery sauce satiating one tired and hungry teacher. My other love – Stracchino. I almost plan my day around it - a squidgy cheese that comes in compact packaging, that just asks to be squodged onto a large hunk of bread. I know the best shops to find it now and tend to walk that way on my return journey from work. There is sometimes a disappointing moment though when I realise that there is no bread in the apartment to squodge it onto which means a five flight scurry to the nearby deli where they sell the Semolina based 'Altamura'. I try not to look disappointed when these run out, as they occasionally do, and accept second best. At the end of the day, as long as the Stracchino gets squodged, it doesn't really matter what it's onto. How about adding a few olives to the mix and some baby artichokes. Sublime and enough to put you off sweet things for life, which is a shame given that Lecce is the home of the sweet thing.

OCTOBER 23rd

My students never fail to bring a smile. Laughter abounds
and it's a delight to see the sense of humour shared – that sense of irony and fun. No explanations needed. Sometimes my lessons are almost too funny. We roll around helplessly, and then I remember, as they do, that they are here to learn English. I've had this sense before, long ago, of feeling as if I'm chatting with friends back home, but in another language and culture. It is an odd sensation, the human condition. Indeed it is the human condition shared, that often sparks such hilarity.

I stroll back from my lessons.

Already dark, there is a strange still to the streets, until I turn a corner onto the main road, where the traffic races past, with no regard for human life. It is tiring to negotiate this road after hours of teaching. I wobble about, trying to stay alert as I wait for the dysfunctional traffic lights to change. This, of course, means nothing, as there are always those who choose to ignore.

I have six lanes to mind, and get caught mid road.

People are passing at the end of the working day, returning home to their families. The air is still warm with an aroma of petrol fumes mixed with the odd waft of Lecce. Lecce has its own smell, like all places. It defines it somehow. A warm, fragrance combined with the traffic fumes. A whiff of danger. A waft of leisure. A scent of flowers that bedeck the balconies. An ownerless dog tootles past, without a care in the world. The shopkeepers chat to each other, gesticulating wildly whilst discussing the injustices of life, their

business, their country, maybe the world. They respond to each other with fervent nods and 'Hai ragiones'. The small market is still open and sells cheeses and meat - great slabs of the stuff. I ask for Pecorino, a cheese I know well. It is different from the type I'm used to and looks very mature, a little like Parmeggiano. I am confused but put it down to ignorance on my part. It is very dark now and the lights of remaining shops glimmer on

impressive shop displays. A rumble of unexpected thunder accompanies my walk. A strike of lightning. An electricity in the air. A headache on the brow. It is very humid and I scurry back to my flat, with my bags and work in tow. On entering my palazzo I see a large family in the doorway. I can tell they are family, just by their facial features and behaviour – from the very old to the very young, they have that instrinsic bond that Italians have.

Do I belong?

I can hear the man who shouts to no one in the street. He shouts with an urgency, as if an oracle of knowledge. Noone is listening. His voice unheard, but echoes round the street. The balconies, festooned with flowers look on with derision, as does the man with the mysterious shop. I don't know what this shop is. It says something about stamps in the window, but I see no stamps. I see a lot of people enter, as if going into a black hole. They never seem to emerge. I wonder what happens there but I don't ask.

You learn very early on not to ask.

OCTOBER 24th

The cat on the balcony below has got it right. He sleeps so peacefully there, surrounded by potted plants, in his cat basket, basking in the sun. Occasionally a paw swipes at some flying creature, but for the most part, he realises there's no need for too much action. I do envy him as my day ahead is pure chaos.

I have seven lessons to perform.

Swinging into action, I head for school and just a couple of lessons later, it's time to poke my head round the door of the luxury take-away where I have discovered the most delicious lunch choice - a pasta and seafood dish, put safely into a carton to be stolled away.

There are plump tiger prawns and squid rings, a little red pepper here, a dash of lemon there, a glaze of parsley on top. This, with a hunk of bread, a few olives, a plum tomato and

lunch is yours. Add a big fat peach to the mix, and you are in a healthy food zone. A squodge of Stracchino is the only naughty element of my meal, but it sits there so sweetly in the fridge, it would be shameful to ignore. After this feast, I am sleepy. I have started to enjoy the odd siesta, given the timing of my day and the warmth of my room so I lie down, ensuring that I've set the alarm at a suitably relaxed pace, and fall asleep for an hour or so. On waking, I take a cup of tea, and pack my school bag. As I

leave the apartment, I scurry down the streets, past the corner bar and the German bank. Outside, as regular as clockwork, stands the patient bank guard. He looks alert but bored. I pass each day, one of several on a rota he waves cheerily to me, almost with relief, as if he is not the only bod around at this dead time of the day, when most Italians are still snoozing.

I'm glad he is there.

It is very quiet at this time of day, almost like midnight, but without the darkness, and I feel safer for him and his colleagues. He is there to protect the bank, but he now has a new job. He's my guardian angel incarnate for 30 seconds every day, until I turn the corner.

OCTOBER 25th

Golden light is bathing my room, and I'm aware that I have left my shutter slightly up. It's

7am and Saturday, so I can enjoy all that Lecce has to offer.

A strong smell of coffee mixed with disinfectant wafts through the apartment. With a brief conversation and resigned air, my flatmates and I discuss our corners of the world. She is nice Laura, and heading back to Naples for a few days - the type of flat-mate you dream about but rarely have.

I head into Lecce, along Via Trinchese towards Piazza Sant'Oronzo, past the street vendors from Africa with their colourful wares and the market to the left, then backtrack, curious about some scarves I see hanging there in silken shades.

I buy a gold based one, all intricate, with hues in harmony. It will go well with everything I've ever had, and some. I notice the plant stall, with small trees and flowers. I want the small palm that sits there in its green pot, but I do not have the will to carry it all the way home. It looks heavy, but still it sits there beckoning to me. The street vendors jostle and joke together, their handbags and scarves, their belts and rugs. I feel saddened but admiring then notice the one selling cooker lighters and approach. His eyes tell me his pain and anguish and he stands apart from the others, in all senses. My heart goes out to him. I buy two. He looks so young. I feel a fool but I buy two.

I can give one to a colleague.

I wonder about this young man and how he came to be here. What happened to him along the way? Sometimes it takes a moment like this, to put us in sharp relief. We know we are lucky, but we don't always feel it. Walking on sadly, I observe the happy family scenes that Italians manage to present so effortlessly - the perfectly dressed children, with whom the handsome father and beautiful mother joke. Some teenagers hang outside a McDonalds. It doesn't please me to see this on the beautiful Baroque landscape. It pleases them though and it pleases McDonalds no doubt. I stroll down Via

Umberto towards Piazza del Duomo, such sublimity surreal. So beautiful. Baroque always. Aesthetics are born in Italians - they live, breathe, create them. Flowers are positioned just so in baskets overhanging shops.

And then I met him.

A dapper young African, with a tweed cap, much like the north of England, and a waistcoat,carrying a pile of slim books. He caught my attention with a smile then engaged me in conversation, asking if I was American or French. No. British, I replied. He told me about

the book. His book. The story of his life and his arrival from Senegal, then his hard years as a street vendor. It was his story and the story of the young man with his gas lighters. I had to have it so I bought a copy.

That evening, I sat and read it, in my flat, until I couldn't keep my eyes open any longer. I was very moved. Poignant stuff. It was tragic yet triumphant. This man had taken a big leap and landed somewhere better. Good for him. To me street vendors were like children, vulnerable and for protection. It would punctuate my time here, my eight months in Lecce.

OCTOBER 26th

A full stretch of a day ahead. I wake up at 5 am with slight headache on the brow, so happy to be off work. It is very peaceful now. The arguing couple sleep, the trumpet player's snoring and no doubt the cat's in dreamland. Only the birds are tweeting and you can hear the shuffle of a slippered neighbour heading somewhere. I lie for a while, reflecting on the week that was. I haven't really had much time to explore so far, and feel slightly guilty about it. There is a claustrophobic element to Lecce, a hemmed in feeling, a slightly dull atmosphere at times. But who can doubt its unrivalled beauty? Who can question its superior class?

I yearn vaguely for the sea. I believe it to be aquamarine, but today I am tired after the week's teaching, so decide to take it easy and wander to the bar on the corner.

There are the glamorous, the well-heeled and the vain. They sit together all peacock in a garden, aloof, loquacious, arrogant. The owner is vexed as usual. He is dealing with the mass selling of cake. They all want them today, great boxfuls of them, for their family gatherings. It's Sunday. The day of family and fun for Italians. All sizes and shapes, all colours and textures, designed to tempt palate and stomach and occasion. Who could believe, how such effort can be put into making these wondrous creations. The tart with the strawberries looks beckoningly at me. I want to succumb but don't. Cake for breakfast? Well why not. I decide it will be for another day.

Sitting quietly, I look at the paper and try to translate as best I can. I'm tired from the week and not up to academia so try to relax but the caffeine puts paid to that. Then I retire to the privacy of my room, and rest. The sunlight bathes everything, even my work. All one glorious glow. My mood slowly lifts so I phone my loved ones for a chat. The echoed voices reassure against a backdrop of street noise which is waking up to the day. The trumpet player begins to practice his songs; the couple below are bickering, I think about a relative; the cat is stretching on its balcony; a woman is cleaning her apartment, hoover on the go; cooking smells commence and garlic wafts around; sheets flutter softly in the warm breeze. I sit on my balcony awhile with a book. It's now midday, and the streets are alive with families, bambini and doglets. The little dogs are sad somehow, the children happy. The adults have a purpose. The family gathering is nigh. The meals are to begin. It's one o'clock and the meals are ready. The doorbells are ringing. The relatives arrive. The laughter and shouting and banter begin. This continues for hours until siesta time. We all fall asleep. Me. The families. The doglets and the cat. Only the birdies keep watch over the city.

Dusk falls inevitably, and I have work to do. I do it with a resigned air. I'd put it off but now I do it. I enjoy it once I start. It's good to see how my students have learned what I have taught them. I like my students. A good thing as a new week begins.

OCTOBER 27th

Heading back to Lecce town centre, I skip down the stairs, past the mysterious man with the briefcase and the old lady with the stick. The sunny ambience lift my spirits instantly, even though I'm lacking sleep. I walk with precision down Via Oberdan towards Piazza Mazzini, with its hotchpotch of stalls, trees and unknown quantities. Beside there are classy shops with their expensive displays, and the landmark Benetton sits squatly at one side.

I weave the fellow pedestrians, the traffic and watch my steps on sometimes rickety pavements. I love to reach Via Trinchese with its air of sumptuous glamour, however vacuous that is. All the big named shops are here as you stroll towards Piazza Sant' Oronzo and the hub of the city. I decide, on this occasion, to have a cappuccino at Alvino's, which is there in the piazza for tourists and locals alike. Its array of sweetmeats is staggering and arresting in its beauty. A tired person can forget routines and I forget that one must get a ticket before the ordering of the drink. I am soon put right and join the ticket queue, beside a large and jolly Italian man. His jocular ways are clearly popular with his friends, and he orders a feast for them, little cakes and all. Tanned cheeks tell of happy times - of seas and boats and travels around, and his pats on the back, show a big heart from a big man. His wife, by comparison, looks quiet and reserved.

She is elegant and fashionable but is wanting for something. This of course is her concern and not ours. I too am wanting something. How easy it is to become demanding in a perfect world. I sit and people watch, a copy of 'Il Quotidiano di Lecce' in hand. The headlines are shocking but I detach from them.

The surface and underneath. Always an interesting thing.

OCTOBER 28th

Incredibly, it's still warm and my days are filled with sunkissed skin as I navigate the Leccese streets towards the shops. I even think of swimming pools as I breeze along the street, yet there are none nearby to my knowledge. Going into the superior delicatessen on Via Oberdan, the charming couple greet me. He engrossed in new stock and she sorting out the wares. There is good reason to enter this shop – in short, their alluring comestibles. Take the Artichokes in pleasing olive oiled jars, or the little pats of cheese. How about the olives or the sundried tomatoes, all plumply scarlet in a bowl. Yet their piece de la resistance, is a thing that lures me there the most - the Altamura panino. This semolina bread is just the thing for squodging good things on. It could be cheese or honey; and matters not a jot. The squidgy squodgy thing is enough reason for me. Every time I pass, I wave, then like a magnet pull, enter the heavenly space of a deli, but one with attitude and class.

I always leave a little happier, and so fairly glide up my palazzo stairs until reaching my flat. And there, having popped said delicacies into the fridge, glide back down, on this occasion almost sliding into Signora Rizzi.

Signora Rizzi, I have come to understand, does not suffer fools gladly. She sees the world in simplest terms, and cannot comprehend otherwise, with rarely a smile on her face, but often a word in her mouth. And so, there she is all newly coiffeured and well-dressed, standing on a stairwell, with bag in hand:

'Ma Signora, why don't you use the lift?'

'Ah, I don't like lifts madam, I prefer to use the stairs. A bit of exercise you see!' My feeble

attempts at humour do little to alter her perspective. I imagine an earthquake would do little too.

'I always use the lift', she states with emphasis on the final word. 'The lift is there to be used'

'Ah', I reply, now a little weary with this petty conversation, 'but it is a question of choice, Signora'.

I then make my excuses and pass quickly down the stairs. Her glance follows me down, as if I am committing some terrible crime. I imagine in her world everything is just so. She wouldn't cope well in another country, I muse - all different and not as it should be. 'Non `e giusto !' must be her favourite words. I've heard them used before, many times.

The warmth pervades and heats the road beneath. I pass, as always, the strange shop which never appears to have customers; the patisserie on the corner and the other bars nearby. As

usual there are people sitting outside, in sunglasses, enjoying the day. You could be forgiven for thinking it's a permanent holiday here.

And then I go past Deutschebank and observe the high buildings on the other side, across Viale Japigia. There seem to be some potted plants and palms up there. I start to wonder if there is a terraced garden, with a pool. In the sticky heat, the thought's seductive.

Then suddenly I notice a strange sight. A man is literally lifting bins. He is huge and smiling as he does so.

There is something quite primeval about it and I'm not sure that I want to head his way. Other people gloss over it, as if a normal occurrence in the mundane world.

As I walk on, I can still perceive the bin lifter far in the distance, all bin lifted up. He appears to be heading back from where he came. Perhaps this was a former job of his, I surmise. Perhaps not.

And then, as if the day is there to spite me, I bump again into Signora Rizzi. She has her busybody face and is no doubt ready to put things right.

'Signora, why are you trying to cross there? There is a better crossing further on'.

Seemingly helpful for a moment, perhaps I've got the lady wrong.

But then the crunch.

'You shouldn't wear those shoes in this heat. You should wear ones like these'.

She is the voice of a super conscience, correcting all that crosses path.

'Grazie Signora' I reply, 'Thanks for your advice'.

And as I stand halfway across the road, mid lane, I hear her shout, 'And you should use the lift!'

Pazienza.

OCTOBER 29th

I read the news today, oh boy. An entire family. Dead. Some bungled robbery.

Looking up at cloudless skies, it doesn't seem right at all. That and the bullet holed walls. The delicate flowerheads of some southern Italian plant seems to nod gently in the breeze, as if to agree.

I try not to dwell on it too much, as I stroll Via Leuca.

The thing that lacks here is water. Sea even.

I had a dream once, many years ago, of a place with fluttering curtained entrance. Striped, red and white. It was on a side street that stretched down to the sea - a shop, I think.

Then another dream.

Imprisoned on the roof of a villa in some hot Mediterranean place.

Imprisoned.

I vaguely recall pacing the roof, all concrete and arid. My captors were there but unseen. I shudder at the thought. Or was it a memory? A previous life even. How can we explain the stories of the night. It was daytime. Very sunny, though not an August heat. I wonder what it meant. Even now, it seems so real.

A throw of light on a pale wall reminds me of the very same.

And back to now ...

The family are no more. Yesterday they had their lives but now they've gone. So transient, life.

The paper juxtaposes this with the fashion and the glamorous.

So Italy.

Another dream once on a large boat. A ferry with seats on the upper deck heading out to sea. And which journey was that I wonder? I don't recall the others. All dignity and mist. Sea mist.

I think of a story about a girl who took a trip to the Amazon. She disappeared within a day and no one knew what became of her. Then years later it seems that she never went there, but instead had been living by the sea in Greece. Noone knew. She'd grown old there and died. Her family had spent years looking through the lens at Brazil. Poor family. Poor girl. Brazil indeed !

Perhaps she didn't like her Sunday crumpets or the nylon sheets of her hometown.

Lecce. All chocolate box with only the hard ones left. And yet it doesn't disappoint. And those moments in our real lives.

I remember that I once had an operation at the age of four on my thumbs. I didn't get it of course. All I knew was the hospital bed and the strange food. Noone explained. Reconstituted egg and orange stuff. Icky medicines and all. Then I slept. When I awoke, all bandaged thumbs, I had no idea what had happened.

'It's magic!' I said to the child in the next bed. She was also perplexed. And then I left sporting blue socks and improved digits.

Life's surprises.

And so it is that I stare at the shop displays and tempting cakes; the warm stones and the light.

Yet underneath lie shifting sands and mystery and murk.

OCTOBER 30th

My students Maria, Anna and I sit in the corner bar near the school. Remarking on places I've seen before, Maria tells me that she'll take me somewhere special if I'd like. I'm intrigued. 'Special in what way?' I enquire. 'A bit spooky,' she says. Perfect for Halloween. And so we arrange to meet in that afternoon.

'It's better at night', she says, 'but we'll go in the afternoon,' Anna laughs and tosses her hair.

Driving through the autumn roads towards Taranto, neither of my Italian friends have told me where this mystery tour will take us.

'You'll love it', they say, laughing.

Good job I'm trusting, I think. So we stop in a village bar to drink an Espresso and nibble on nuts before proceeding on our way.

The birds perched here and there seem an omen of some sort. Creepy, I think. They've set the scene. And so we drive and still I guess. Is it an old part of Taranto? No. Is it Matera with its bat caves? No. Still they hold it in and then, finally we stop the car. At first I see nothing of note, then Anna point up a hill.

'Craco!' She says.

Craco, she tells me hasn't been lived in since 1963. As I look up at the town, I believe it. Small dark squares form vacant windows attached to eerie old buildings. The windows seem to watch us back and you sense a thousand ghostly eyes following you. They moved out, she explains, due to unsustainable land and other problems. An entire population left. All that culture abandoned. Gone for eternity. And so we sit and watch and scare each other a little

Maybe there are ghosts up there, jokes Maria.

Perhaps if we walked around, doors would clank behind us and we'd be trapped there forever, giggles Maria.

'They do tourist visits there,' said Anna, but not this time of year. Now it's all deserted.

It seems the town dates back to the iron age though oldest remains are Norman.

'It's been used for films,' said Maria. 'Big ones. James Bond.'

'I can believe,it,' I grin.

The sky seems to glower for a while over the hilltop town. Blackened windows seem to threaten us and yet beckon us too.

'Shall we go up?', says Anna

'No' says Maria, 'You need a guide'

Anna talks of the time she and her friends did just that.

'We were young and foolish,' then she said. 'Teenagers.'

She says that nothing happened, except the strange and eerie noises of the wind through hollowed buildings and the creaky slam of a door. The wind, only the wind.

'Let's go back now.' says Anna 'It's giving me the creeps'

We all agree. And as we drive, I look up at the forlorn town and swear I can see the ghosts of people by the old walls.

The drive back to Lecce sees us quiet as mice. Glad we did that, we agree, but not at night.

We laugh.

OCTOBER 31st

Oh bejeezers, it's Halloween today and I still haven't got the stuff - the little chocolates shaped like pumpkins and the coloured paper for the kids. With a harried air, I rush to the relevant shops, after a speedy breakfast at the down -to -earth bar, and buy absurd amounts

of Halloween themed paraphernalia. It is celebrated here as much as home, so must be done.

Arriving at my kids' class, I am met with the resigned look of your average child. They have clearly had a day of Halloween already, and are a bit jaded with the whole thing. However, most of them warm to the task of creating a Halloween-themed poster with a fun theme of witchiness. That is, apart from Rosella, who looks bored and above the idea. A little older than the others, she's clearly not amused. As she examines her nail polish, and refuses to stoop so low, an unpleasant atmosphere ensues, with the other children trying to rally her round.

Meeting her half-way, I ask if she'd prefer to do some English book exercises and she's happy with this. I see that childhood has come to an early finish for this young lady and feel saddened by it. The tiniest children enjoy it though and they laugh and scream and gurgle with delight, whilst demolishing the chocolate pumpkins. This seems to meet the approval of young Mario, who is much happier playing with his orange truck whilst eating said pumpkin chocolate. He doesn't go in for this English nonsense though. Whatever next! Little Graziella has started to annoy wee Simona though and tries to poke her cardboard broom into her compatriot's ear. Meanwhile, Simona is not happy about this and begins to throw her dolly around with abandonment. This does not please young Mario who is enjoying his orange truck time, and does not wish to be disturbed. The joys of teaching small children!

As I wander back home to my flat, children's laughter everywhere, as they scurry about doing Italian 'Trick or Treat' with their parents.

Ah, the peace and quiet of my apartment.

A delicious meal of Tuna pasta and a small squodge of Stracchino. A Camomile tea. Lovely. Time for bed. So nice to snuggle under the duvet and fall asleep with only the gurgling of the pipes for company. But, oh no, the student party in the opposite flat is just warming up for the night, and the shouts and whoops are in full flow out on their balcony...

CHAPTER TWO – NOVEMBER

NOVEMBER 1st

I have a four day holiday and the streets lie temporarily deserted. For a while, I lie in bed wondering what to do with my time. I have a lot of work but a little voice tells me that I must rest.

Wandering out onto the balcony I see the lazy cat lying prostate on its throw. It looks at peace with the world and a beautiful day ensues. Before too long, I start to hear the merry voices of Italian children chattering on the street and the deep resounding laughter of two old men. People are beginning to wake up to the day and enjoy it. I contact my friend Maria and we arrange to meet up for a coffee at 10.30 am.

It is brilliant, out there by the corner bar, to see her strolling towards me with her trademark beam. We enter the cafe for a quick

Espresso, before heading off in her car towards San

Cataldo. The streets are beginning to fill with merry makers and the

odd car hoots at a friend.

As we travel along the old road, I am absorbed by the scenery – the

many trees and plants,

the last traces of summer still visible and the autumn sun shining on a faded palazzo here,

an old shop there. We chat animatedly of this and that, enjoying the company and the

drive. She points out landmarks as we go and I delight in seeing everything for the first

time. When we arrive at San Cataldo, it's already brimming with people, mostly locals

on a day out, looking out to sea or walking along the promenade. Primary coloured boats

bob on the waves and an enthusiastic dog races by, nearly knocking us over. We talk

awhile about our lives, our past and our present and take snapshots with our camera

phones. My battery has run out, so Maria comes to the rescue and takes some shots for

me. Then we walk into a nearby bar for a cappuccino, and she tells me about her

childhood spent with family and the early jobs.

We share common experiences of school and early disappointments,

reflecting philosophically on the lives we went on to lead. As we

leave the cafe, a sudden gust of wind ruffles our hair and we realise

that we are quite cold. We stay awhile, looking out to sea, but

then head towards the car. A well dressed couple walk in front of us.

He has an air of arrogance and superiority, she one of entitlement.

Every stitch is perfect, an ironing dream.

The trouser length is just so, the tailored jackets on their backs, a glittering jewel here, a costly watch there. Her hair is blonde, though not naturally so and his grey flecked. They communicate little to each other and exude an air of tension. I wonder what their home is like. I guess they may have more than one. Perhaps a secluded villa somewhere near Porto Cesareo, an apartment in Milan. I wonder what they do for a living. I guess that she works in some capacity with clothing as she has fashionista's perfect attention to detail and he is a businessman with one in every town. I imagine their children- perfect specimens, in their teens and early twenties, with lavish rooms and all the latest that technology can buy. I muse

that one daughter will be a model, whilst the other will follow her mother into the business side of the fashion industry. A son will be a businessman like his father but maybe he will break the mould and go to university, become a lawyer or a doctor. They are your typical well-heeled Italian couple and for me represent for me modern Italy, though they have no idea. Their posh dog follows them obediently to the name of Sergio. He jumps into the back of their car, with a comfortable air, having made the trip a million times whilst a young couple pass with two small children in tow. The little boy is quite naughty and father repeatedly scolds him.

He's a character.

The little girl is sweet and well-behaved in comparison. She holds her mamma's hand and looks on her brother's antics with a vague derision. An elderly couple walk by, with slightly sad expressions. To see a couple without children is poignant somehow. Of course their children may have lived around the corner and be waiting for them, but it struck me how unusual it is to see a small family unit in Italy. Across the road are some young ragazzi having fun. The girls laugh coquettishly as the boys, joke and lark about. All dark and good-looking, the girls are linking arms, and chatting gaily about their young lives. An air of joy and optimism bounces off them all. A young man races by on his Vespa, trying to impress

the young girls around. He pulls up a verge and tosses his curly dark

mane back off his face.

He's wearing dark sunglasses and a leather jacket. Confident, if a

little uneasy at the same time. Perhaps he realises that there is a time

and a place for this peacock behaviour, and it

isn't now. A gentle ambience pervades the atmosphere,a rising heat,

a more intense sun.

Maria puts on her radio and I hear Italian voices. The music is a

perfect accompaniment to stunning views; late autumn flowers;

palms; villas and olive groves. All have their place here in modern

Italy - the billboards with colourful logos and the birds that hop on

them.

All belong here.

It starts to rain a little, so we look for a quiet trattoria to have our lunch. A very rotund waiter, called Mario, appears to take our order. He is slightly breathless from the orderings and the comings and goings. We order a bottle of water and he brings us some local bread. It has chilli pepper in. Hot. I'm not sure I want this right now, so just nibble at a piece to be polite. I decide, on a second perusal of the menu, to order Spaghetti all'Arrabbiata. Peasant food says Maria. Delicious food say I. And it is.

Mario brings it and Maria's pasta alla Frutta di Mare, with rosy cheeked joviality. His bushy

moustache seems to have a life of its own, I reflect. The waiter scuttles to and fro like a plump clockwork toy, with his whiter than white jacket and his blacker than black trousers. I try out my Italian on him and he seems to understand, so that's good. Both Mario and Maria indulge me like a child. I feel satisfied with myself. Satiated. Happy.

NOVEMBER 2nd

The holiday continues in earnest and I lie in bed thinking about the lovely day had yesterday and the meal at Mario's. The rickety grinding of the shutters lifting on the day reveals leaden clouds and impending rain, so I reflect a moment on how to spend it. I decide to go into Lecce and have a mooch around the shops. Trotting along quiet streets, it begins to rain heavily. Very soon it is Monsoon and quite alarmingly so. Stupidly I've forgotten my umbrella, but this is hardly a problem as the African street vendors have them in all colours, like deflated balloons. The locals huddle everywhere in shop doorways avoiding all contact with the huge drops. I'm both amused and a little frightened by this, as if they know something I don't, though the street vendors carry on regardless, dripping goods in their hands, with faces undeterred. One stops me near the supermarket and tries to sell me a leather belt. I explain that I don't really need one, and they are quite expensive, but I

might get one before Christmas. I want to give him something, some smidgeon of hope.. I walk along a now deserted Via Trinchese, wet leaden walkways guiding my way. A Vespa whizzes round the corner, nearly knocking me over, making me tense. Waiting at the traffic lights, I buy a tartan umbrella from another street vendor. People observe disapprovingly. It seems we are supposed to ignore. I ignore. I like to make my own decisions. I'm not a sheep.The waft of coffee wins me over so I enter a corner bar that I haven't visited before. It's cosy inside, away from the rain. A red-chequered table cloth reminds me of a very distant past. I hug my cappuccino with wet fingers and realise that I feel a little cold. Looking at the patisserie section of the bar, a large plump Cornetto stares back at me with oozing custard. It is lightly sprinkled with icing sugar and placed next to several others on a doily with a gleaming metal tong. A slim Italian couple enter the bar. They are extremely glamorous and order one each, along with an Espresso. This, I decide, gives me carte blanche to order one too. Perhaps I am a sheep after all. The Cornetto squidges and squodges but itsticky sweetness says something. It seems everyone has one so, in a guilty kind of way, we share this pleasurable moment. The only downside, the aftermath. The dabbing ofthe flakes, the squoozling of the stickiness. Onwards into the town. A small, white fluffy dog yaps at another smaller dog whilst I negotiate another six-laned road and a family hurry by with Benettoned kids. An old man stumbles along the road, looking sad and confused and some Carabinieri drive by in their black and red uniforms, looking cool. They are laughing at some joke and seem to enjoy life. Soon I reach Piazza Sant'Oronzo. It is quiet but only in the centre where cafes are brim with locals and tourists, then wander to the Roman amphitheatre and reflect a moment on how it must have been, shuddering at the thought of gladiators and the like. I buy some postcards, take some photos then explore a small antique market and buy a book before strolling towards the magnificent Duomo, with its crazy guy on the steps. Entering the atmospheric gloom, I marvel like a tourist. The gilded Baroque. The frescoes. The different levels.

A polite man takes a fee then I leave and feel the rain again before scurrying to the tourist office. I like it here. It's full of books and posters about Lecce and its selection of postcards particularly good. I enter Duomocafe. An arrogant family play tyrant with the staff who bite their lip and soldier on.

Two old women, like birds of prey, sit gossiping to one side. They are the self righteous. They know it all with their dyed blonde hair and darker roots... The rain is heavier and I sit awhile, pondering on Lecce so far. It has been a month and I almost feel at home now. There is a claustrophobic atmosphere, but it's a beautiful place, without question. Without questions. I have a thousand, but don't ask.

NOVEMBER 3rd

It's 4 am and I'm wide awake. I can hear the peculiar ghostly sound that comes from somewhere. Maybe animal, maybe thing. I can't tell, but it spooks the living daylights out of me. It's very quiet this time of day, save spooky thing, and even the shouting greeters are in slumber.

I've noticed a temperature drop, but only by a degree or so. Nothing major. I realise my bedding will be insufficient soon. A flimsy sheet and light quilt will hardly do the job. I have been in Italy mid winter and it really does get cold, and so I make it the day's mission to find myself some suitable bed wear.

Trip tropping along Via Trinchese, having narrowly avoided Signora Rizzi who happened to be admonishing another at the time, I walk along the streets, past Benetton; past the market and past the Bank of Napoli. But just before, I see the shop I'm looking for with beautiful display of all things duvet. Inside I go. Suctioned into the zone that is all things bed, a couple assist. Perhaps a little too friendly, oppressive even..

What kind or size or style? This one or that? This would be perfect, they say, or that. I can't look around in peace. They will decide for me. With convincing patter, if I have this I will also need that. If I don't have that, I will freeze in winter. If I don't have this precise type, it will be unbearable. I'll have to get the plane home then, I grin inwardly! And so, three Euros short of a hundred, I part the shop, a lot more laden, and a lot less Euroed.

I feel a bit silly as I stagger along the road, with duvet; a fresh sheet and two plump pillows to boot. People look at me as if I have five heads. The Gorgon or something. The huge pink Gorgon monster. Perhaps if I look at them, they will turn to stone and 'lasciarmi in pace'.

Sadly not. They stare and they stare. Ridiculous, I feel. Have they not seen a small woman loaded up with bedding striding along Via Trinchese before ? What's wrong with them!

And so the approach to my flat, I feel exhausted and daft in equal measure. Luckily, I don't have the added bonus of seeing Signora Rizzi. I'm sure she would have forced me into the lift with these. A quick push and I'd be wedged in the corner for eternity.

After a cup of tea, I replace the inadequate bedding. It does look pleasingly sleep inducing, and so I feel that all the pain of my experience was worth it in the end. At least I hope so.

That evening, after my lessons, I return with renewed enthusiasm to my bed and almost gulp my tea to try it out. How will it be?

The night is hot and sticky. Humid. The bedding far too warm yet, and so that night the shiny new covers are placed back in my wardrobe and I lie underneath one inadequate sheet to catch up on sleep, then the rains arrive.

NOVEMBER 4th

It's Tuesday morning and a peachy light greets me at dawn. The rain hasn't abated yet and my neighbours' pot plants are completely drenched along with my drying clothes. There's a slight chill in the air and the prospect of the shower appeals less. I have decided to spend some time working today, catching up on chores and planning for the week ahead. The buzzer goes. I am a little nervous, as I can't imagine who it is. A familiar voice booms out, ''Sono io, Signore Rovere'. It's the landlord. What on earth does he want at this ungodly hour? I perceive other voices. Good grief, how many people are there out there? I'm barely up, so open the door, twisting the metal locks with precision There stands he and a cast of thousands - a band of flat hunters, seeking to explore our place They invade the zone, barely engaging or exchanging eye contact, and want to see my room. Oh no! I am aghast.

Books and clothes lie everywhere. A wet towel drapes over the radiator. At least I can place my new pink bedding all plump and clean. Like a child covering its eyes to hide, I decide to leave them to it. Unseen shame is preferable I surmise. My flat is searched and appraised like a defunct washing machine. I play Dodgems. One minute, I'm making a

tea, the next I'm in the bathroom. My flatmates are lucky as away for the holiday

weekend.

Almost in a thrice, they are gone. The landlord looks back as he leaves, 'Mi

raccomando...' I don't catch the last few words, but I know it wasn't great. I bury

myself in work to forget, to move on.

The rain has paused and I need some air. Feeling hemmed in, I enter the world,

appreciating the slight chill in the air. The greengrocers seem appealing right now so I

enter the den that is theirs and admire the plump fresh vegetables and fruit; the jars

containing preserves; strings of nuts and exotic prodotti. The baby artichokes are hard to

resist sitting like green goblins in a jar. I buy these, a panino and some milk. They don't

have cheese but for Ricotta and Mozzarella. These are the ones you are supposed to

want, but I want Stracchino or Gorgonzola.They have neither, nor Pecorino. I feel a bit

deflated and buy Tuna instead, and a big fat peach. It's lunch time and I'm feeling

peckish. The invasion has built me an appetite. An angry man shouts at his wife, 'Mai,

mai, mai!' I don't know what will never happen. I don't know what will happen. I don't

know and right now I don't care. All I care about is my lunch and a cup of tea.

NOVEMBER 7th

I've decided that it's time to pay my first visit to a local hairdresser's. This will be a new

experience for me here in Lecce, and I'm not blessed with time. I've spotted a few near

my flat, and one has particularly caught my attention, opposite the friendly vegetable

shop. I enter with trepidation, an intense shyness overcoming me. There are three

women working there, each with the trademark glossy locks of a perennial hairdresser. I explain that I want to go darker, thus nearer to my natural colour. This all seems fine, although I soon realise I'm not exactly au fait with hairdressing vocabulary, and even the simplest instructions become a minefield. We seem to approach an understanding so I sit dumbly

but optimistically in my chair. The assigned hairdresser buffets me around like a child pointing hither and thither with a 'qua' and a 'la'. A shampoo so quick it would suit a ferret, with the obligatory tuts about the sorry state of my mop. I feel rather affronted but gagged by my lack of hair terminology all the same. A towel draped around my shoulders, the ladies talk amongst themselves and with their regulars, of their lives and annoyances, of this and that. A joke here and there, goes over my head. I sit like a stuffed cabbage awaiting my next instruction. A gloopy mix is applied to my head, with foils and towels to seal it in. I notice that it's raining heavily outside again, which so often happens, I muse, when at the hairdressers. Trying to engage in conversation with my hairdresser, my Italian's not bad so we can converse. She talks to me as if to a child, with exaggerated vowels, then turns to the adults for the real conversation. I feel a little silly, sitting there. A magazine appears on the table in front of me so I pick it up and flick through slowly. Suddenly a flash of lightning illuminates the shop and seems a precursor to heavy rain. The radio plays in the background with singers I'm not familiar with whilst a small child appears, belonging to one of the workers. He plays with a toy and is gently scolded by his mother for touching the products. An hour later and I'm still there. Still one stuffed cabbage wearing foil cap and feeling a fool. Suddenly, I am ushered to a sink, 'Vieni, vieni', to have the dye washed off. Words of approval echo from the ladies present, heralding another success story in their colouring department history. I am taken back to my chair. Che orrore! My hair is practically black. I'm not blaming the hairdressers for this, as it is probably some linguistic miscommunication, but I feel inwardly crestfallen and crushed. I am pale skinned and blue-eyed, so the effect is more Emo than sophisticate - a harsh look, and not one I wished for. I try not to cry, being a little tired and all, but put on a brave face and pretend to like, so as not to offend. They look pretty pleased with themselves. A fait accompli. They are not too perceptive as

they don't notice my discomfort. Perhaps the rains will wash it lighter, I fantasise. I pay them. It's a reasonable price so I'm thankful at least for that. They practically prevent my exit, not for sinister reasons, but to protect me from the rain. The outside road is now a river. At least I am heading back to my flat and not to work. I just know I will be completely drenched. I wonder at life's moments - the ones you'd have been better not to bother with - and decide to brave the drops, hairdressers aghast. When I say wading home, I don't exaggerate. Italians huddle in shop doorways, none venturing out. Drivers spray the pavements as they speed by. It is a dismal five minutes. Superficial and inward gloom in

complete harmony. Arriving at my palazzo, two old ladies tut in disapproval. 'Ma Signora, sei bagnata'. Yes I'm well aware I'm wet and just thankful they didn't add, 'and your hair looks awful'.

Be grateful for small mercies. Perhaps if I wash it a lot, it will fade more quickly. I have a feeling that it won't. I enter my apartment, dripping everywhere. Vanity supersedes comfort as I examine my hair in every mirror, my breath clouding each one. I can't escape the fact that I don't like it. I don't like it at all. Later on that day, I enter my corner bar. I am so embarrassed and might as well have three heads and a gonk perched

on there. Familiar locals stare. The barmaid with the funky punky haircut likes it, but

she would, as it's so extreme. This embarrassment is nothing compared to work later that

day. I have kind students. Even the teenagers are clearly surprised, but try not to show it.

A few compliment me kindly, but I am ashamed. I have a black monstrosity on my head.

Courage required, I have my youngest class-the pre-schoolers. They do not mince their

words.

'Why is your hair black now?' Asks young Mario with a disapproving glance. It is hard

to answer this simple question. I offer, 'Because I've been to the hairdresser's today

Mario'.

'But why did you do that?' he enquires. My thoughts hover somewhere around 'Because

I'm a silly idiot, who should know better.' Thank goodness for tomorrow. After a sleep,

maybe I'll have come to terms with the fact that I now have a laughing gorilla on my

noggin!

NOVEMBER 8th

It's 4 am and I can hear the strange caw cawing of an Italian bird, species unknown.

Apart from this there is an unusual silence and a peaceful vibe. It really stands out as so

rare to have such a moment in Lecce, indeed in Italy. In fact, silence would be strange in

this world, and a little unnerving were it later in the day, save siesta time. I potter into the

kitchen to have a very early morning cup of tea. A small saucepan on the old oven, gas

lighter at the ready. It soon starts to bubble away, to that magical point where you know

it will make a good cup then I return to my room, with the delicious brew, and climb

back into bed to think about things. I like to reflect and plan at this time and find a clarity to my thoughts that sets me up for the day. It's a little nippy, but nothing to write home about, so I put on a cardigan and settle back down. After a while, I decide to get up and have a shower. The other two flatmates are still asleep so I try not to disturb. I can hear someone leaving the palazzo, on their way to work, and a car door slam, then the rowing couple wake up and

don't disappoint. I wonder why they stay together, though I'm sure parting would not be so easy, for a number of reasons. Sometimes I can hear their grandchildren there, and laughter, even joy in their voices, but then once they've left, the bad humours return and the moaning and bickering resume. At 8 am I pop down to the corner bar for a cappuccino. The regulars are yet to come, but some early risers join me. The owner looks weary already, the bar staff stressed. He barks orders at them and they try not to react, though clearly annoyed. Mrs. Owner arrives and presents a calming vibe. A better mood starts to prevail. She smoothes the edges and soothes frayed tempers.

NOVEMBER 9th

Wandering lazily through the door of my flat, I can hear voices inside. This perplexes me as the others are away. Who can it be? With trepidation, I open the door to see four very tall and glamorous people standing in my kitchen. One explains. The nipote of the landlord and they are to stay here for the night.

Models they are, from Bari doing a catwalk the next day,and so it is that I lose my place for 24 hours to gay laughter and the squatting of the bathroom. I don't recall even making it in there so busy it was.

Have you ever felt so small as to no longer exist?

I often wish so when I see Signora Rizzi, but this is different. I feel so small, that they might walk through me. Am I here any more?

I repair to school. My lessons are as planned and the small ones are suitably childish.

'Why do we have to sing silly songs?' asks Mario.

'To improve our English' I reply efficiently.

'Why don't we just speak English then?' The small one enquires.

'Because it's more fun this way' I reply.

'It's not fun' Replies Mario.

'Yes it is' retorts Maria. Ah well, I have some allies after all, and they're smaller than me.

And thus I return to the tall ones.

Returning to my flat, across the six-laned road, I wonder if I'll get squished today. It seems a suitable end to my day. As it happens, I don't get flattened today, but merely reduced again by the incredible height of my flat sharing squatters. By now they've even taken root in the kitchen. While one is cooking another is in the tub. Whilst one is in the tub, another is cooking. How I long for tomorrow! And so I enter the room. My room. At least they haven't taken up residence in here. Yet.

I climb into my sheetiness and sleep a sleep, with one eye open and one ear shut. Uneasy.

The morning sees me escaping to the corner bar. I wave to the friendly veg shop couple, though wonder why my face expresses joy. Perhaps I'm learning the art of bella figura. And then, I enter the bar, and see the familiar staff, harassed but polite as ever.

Sitting down with jam-filled Cornetto and frothing Cappuccino, I decide to escape all things aesthetically pleasing into 'Il Quotidiano'.

It was suitably grim.

Another day's worth of criminal faces staring from the page.

At least I have some space but then in they all come. All eyes turn of course. They order with panache and chat amongst themselves. The good news is that they are soon gone, to the catwalk world and I am left with my teeny weeny world all small and light.

Lovely.

NOVEMBER 10th

Six am and I hear the caw cawing of the bird. Another day ahead of lessons and songs, no doubt infused with some Stracchino.

And so I do my ablutions in peace at last, and make my way down endless stairs, almost tripping in my enthusiasms. Other inhabitants are leaving their apartments; some with children, many not and I leave the palazzo to a slightly overcast day. Mooching about the nearby bins, I spot the bin lifter doing his thing.

Sometimes I wish I could give him my shopping to do; so keen he is for all things heavy. I see the grumpy bar goer. He's hardly a worry, but does manage to wipe the smiles and dull the day.

I have a speedy Espresso then make my way to the launderette with my latest offerings .

The two ladies are there as ever, as if for eternity, focused and absorbed in their work. Mindfulness.

One greets me and takes my stuff and, for a moment, I pause to see the giant whirring and whooshing of ancient machines; the hiss of a press.

My lessons pass without incident and I can return to my flat to rest awhile. I've managed to plan ahead and the angst of the day is diluted some. And so it is, I finally succumb to a proper snooze, after a quick pasta dish infused with garlic and parsley. Sleepily, I reach for my phone at 3 pm. It's time for work again. Heading down the stairs once again, trip tropping all pony as I go, I see two things. Firstly, a large sign on the lift-'Out of order' and secondly, Signora Rizzi who's holding a small bowed dog. The dog's shivering in her arms and I wonder how many times the poor mite's been party to the lift.

She points at the metal monstrosity. 'It's broken.'

'Ah yes, I see.'

She looks quite angry as she delivers her verdict on the malfunctioning machine.

'It is because people don't use it enough. If they used it, it would work!' She explains.

'It is like a car without petrol', she adds. 'No petrol. No go'.

I fail to see her argument so nod feebly in the awnings of the ingresso, trying to make sense of such petty thoughts. Fettered like a doomed beast, I stand awhile listening to her arguments and observe the two pursed lips and the shivery dog.

Luckily at that moment, another lucky resident enters the frame and I am free to go, as she delivers the news to the hapless one

And then, as if to defy logic, she shouts to me,

'Do not use the lift!'

Convinced she's perhaps not the full shilling, I go on my way, thanking the stars for my escape. And so I walk the cracked pavements and teeter amidst the six-laned road, whilst waving to the bank guard, until I realise this could be misconstrued as directing traffic. Finally across, I see a large intimidating man. This one, I was told is, alright really although there was once the small matter of a multiple murder and a long spell 'inside'.

I'll call him Harb for brevity. (He's alright really but...) Seeing Harb is further reason not

to enter lifts, I muse. Perish the thought.

Another day in Lecce.

NOVEMBER 11th

Returning from morning lessons, arms full of books and shopping regalia, I finally open

the giant portone and enter the ingresso. Unfortunately I'm so wrapped up in my thoughts

that I fail to notice Signora Rizzi behind me. At that very moment a family also enter the

scene. Picture the plump couple and their podgy offspring all fattened liked some

Christmas birds.

The man is red-cheeked and huffs and puffs his way to the lift whilst the wife follows

meekly behind with two chubby kids. The button pressed and so comes the rattly

metallic box. My first thought is that they can't all fit in yet somehow, like squeezing

large tent into small bag, they push and they bend until all are wedged inside. To my

astonishment, this does not deter Signora Rizzi, who also insists on entering the frame.

More sparrow than marrow, the tiny lady clamps in all papier mache. So five sets of

limbs and five blushing cheeks can be seen swallowed up by the metal pulley of the lift

and I begin to wonder how long the oxygen would last in there, were it to break down

now. Those five flights of stairs have never looked so good! I have no further lessons

today so decide to wander to the market and take a proper look. November, yet still mild,

I take a jacket and head along Via Oberdan to Piazza Mazzini before crossing the busy

road to Via Trinchese.

'Cesare!' Barks a man, at his misbehaving pooch. 'Mi raccomando!' The dog seems none the wiser.

I grab a Cappuccino near the market on the high stools by the bar and read the paper. Then I look at the stall, with their trinkets piled high, a million shades of everything – a mosaic of colours. A peaceful ambience pervades and gentle vibe. Not much haggling, the stall holders seems more inert than alert to some great deal.

I don't buy much save a cheap jumper that will do for chilly nights ahead then proceed through the town's main square right along to Via Vittorio Emanuelle. I've seen a small trattoria. Cheap and unostentatious, it doesn't shout out to you but has a rustic charm. Entering and down some steps, I find I am alone. The room is dark; a simple unfussy affair, all chequered cloth.

I'm shown to my table then given the menu. The food lacks sophistication and this appeals, so old favourites such as Carbonara on the list.

I choose a 'Penne all'Arrabbiata' with side salad and freshly baked Italian breads. Starting to nibble on this, I'm nearly full by the time my meal arrives. A dessert spoon of Parmigiano sprinkled over and then the first bite. Happily, delicious. Piquante, the chilli just so, a hint of garlic, even Parsley. The crimson sugo coats al dente pasta, each morsel a delight, then the bread to soak the juices . A crunchy salad takes Balsamic nicely and a little salt. I eat it all then look again at the menu. Recently I've eaten fruit, but this time I'm for the creamy Tiramisu. It arrives all inviting in tall glass with coffee amaretto at its base. I taste the delicious thing. A coffee spray melds with the cream and graces every spoon. The moreish dessert is soon gobbled and I wipe my lips. Espresso to follow on. All sharp and energizing.

And so this cheap yet tasty meal meets my approval and I know to return here sometime. As I re-enter the street, I must adjust my eyes to a blinding light, then I stroll the back streets and admire the old town with its elegant apartments, garden terraces and wrought iron on the balconies, all ornate, where people hub to eat or chat. The November sun overhead seems to kiss each one.

I imagine the lives lived there, all family and tightknit -the cousins and the uncles; bambini and nonnas – all interwoven and tied.

Then I head back slowly, along Via Trinchese. The street is lined with vendors selling bags. Here and there, you are approached with this trinket or that. Beggars sit, lean or lurch, forlorn and desperate, in the shadows of glamour and cut a sad picture.

On the way back I go to Dok, to stock up with some food. I buy a pat of Gorgonzola and Italian bread; some vine tomatoes and a few stuffed olives then a pack of pasta and chilli paste.

Returning to my flat, I stroll down Via Oberdan. It's quiet. Siesta time by now and the families are a lunching. The streets seems strange at this time – all Marie Celeste. Yet they're all indoors, enjoying a snooze, or maybe a late lunch.

I enter through my giant portone and look at my mail box. These are old, perhaps some fifty years and so I see the names of residents gone by and other times.

I'm blessed as Signora Rizzi is nowhere to be seen. Just the reserved couple from three floors down and as we pass I realise there is a timeless feel. It could be 1955. The old light fittings and the ancient lift; the wooden mail boxes and crucifix on a wall. All old-fashioned and gentile.

Finally, cocooned in the warmth of my flat, I take my leave of Lecce. Closing my eyes, I see delicious plates of food and tiny dogs; pastel apartments and flowery balconies; old-fashioned lifts and mailboxes. Sleep.

NOVEMBER 12th

Sometimes when I stare up at the ceiling in my flat and see whitewashed walls, a cross on one, a painting to the left, I'm reminded of some years ago when I fell ill with a female complaint and was rushed to hospital.

Siena, Italy. This beautiful town with its medieval centre and towers; its undulating hills and trees.

And so I lay in a hospital bed – a ward of ten. The others came and went. Delirious at first, the walls and bed and light melded into one. The doctor would come once a day to check on things and every day a new injection into the derriere. I remember each day, the same meal of meat and spinach. Spinach and meat. It became difficult to swallow. And so I'd lie and watch and wait; the walls oppressive in intense heat.

Three weeks I lay there. Three long weeks. I'd wake up early to the routine of bed bath and jab then lie long hours until the lunch, then Visiting, then tea. I couldn't sleep as all I did was doze. Then the noise of other patients, some in pain. I'd stare across at a wooden cross, there on a white wall or look up at the high white ceiling, projecting stories and films to amuse myself. After three weeks I could leave and recall the hospital departure to brilliant light and intense heat. July it was.

When I look up at my ceiling, I remember that and how we take so much for granted. And so I leave the flat and head down sunny streets towards the school, laden as ever.

Reaching the corner bar opposite my school, I engross myself in 'Il Quotidiano di Lecce'. I am translating a story about agriculture and working with a tricky verb when suddenly I hear a voice in my ear.

Ernesto.

This time he's not talking but singing! His eyes dance with mischief as he serenades, 'Dimmi quando, quando, quando'. For a moment, I have to pinch myself, being half asleep, but realise this is really happening. The other bar goers turn a blind eye and humour the old man whilst the bartender winks at the fun of it all. Then, after a verse or two, she scolds him a little, 'Ernesto! La Signora wants to be left in peace.'

Like a guilty schoolboy, he warbles to a close and drinks his drink and then apologizes for five minutes. 'Mi dispiace Signora.'

I smile in forgiveness and bid him good day before tripping on uneven stones outside. The lurching onto pavement is hardly dignified, but I'm uninjured and soon find myself facing the teashop. Not only that, but a small box of Baci. It looks appealingly back at me and so, unusually, I find myself buying the naughty things to eat at break.

After my teenage lessons, the last one gone, I sit to eat a few of the delicacies, all encased in silver and blue. They are morsels of deliciousness and soon gobbled. I then head down to the corner bar, hoping that Ernesto isn't there.

He isn't but to my consternation Harb is outside pestering a tiny bird-like old woman. It's most peculiar. Like some bizarre mating ritual, he dances this way, she hops that. They bicker. He teases. He tries to scare here, big ghoul that he is. I'm appalled but helpless to do much about it and wonder as to their relationship. They clearly know each other. Perhaps his mother-in-law? Who knows! And so with a Baci still sweetening my mouth, I watch this horror, before returning to the school with one takeaway Espresso. That evening, as I negotiate all tippy toed the uneven pavements towards my flat, I wonder what will come next. Will it be Ernesto singing, 'Vedrai, vedrai' or a giant ghoul chasing a tiny old woman; or will I have the pleasure of bumping into Signoral Rizzi by the lift?

Chissa!

NOVEMBER 13th

As I walk towards the school again there's the reassuring sight of one bank guard who waves to me across the slatted sunlit street. True to form, and not far behind, the bin lifter is lifting bins, though this time with a toy in one hand, perhaps a doll. He sways it precariously, this way and that, whilst with the other scooping up a big one, doubtless full of rubbish. I never see anyone with him and wonder how he lives; probably with family but let out for the day, I surmise, to do his thing.

Popping to the mini supermarket, I try to buy some fruit but there stands the patient assistant dealing with a thousand old ladies, all with stern intent. I guess that Signora Rizzi would be one of them were she not elsewhere. As this one and that gives precise orders to the harried man, I decide not to add to his burden and forego for the bar to see the teachers but then I spot the tiny bird-like lady, pass this way and that outside a bar. I don't see Harb, but I see she is perturbed. She enters and orders a drink then leaves again before it's made. A beautiful, sunny afternoon, we decide to sit outside. The tiny old woman approaches us in haste, 'Signora, Signora. That man is scaring me.'

She stands close by, seeking our protection, but there's no man in sight and tells us anxiously some disjointed story which makes no sense to us and so we soothe and sympathise without understanding fully the situation. When we ask the bartender if she knows, we are stonewalled. Nothing is explained.

'Oh, she's a little crazy,' she says. We are upset, but really have no grounds or way to help and so try to calm and send her home.

In the distance, we see one tiny frightened sparrow lady muttering in the street. She zigzags past the shops and enters some like a clockwork mouse then scurries out again, all anxiety and stress.

It saddens us but we feel helpless. My kiddie lesson sees us dancing around the tiny room and learning animals. And so I learn that one small boy lives on a farm with cows. He goes down on all fours to demonstrate the ways of the mooing beasts. The others giggle and I interject where possible with the word 'cow' and then they sit quietly to draw the farmyard beasts including a plump pig by a rabbit hutch, and one that is Peppa pig. In this childish world, I lose myself and try to forget frightened little bird-like ladies and giant toy wielding bin lifters and wonder at life's eccentrics.

Much later, after lessons, sees me along those pavements to my road. A couple are sitting there, slightly down a lane, talking intimately. She's all glammed up and he in working suit. I see them kiss, then guiltily he turns to see who saw. The car's engine rumbles awhile, but soon it purrs out from the side street and stolls away. I'm ready for my bed. Drinking warm milk, I lie staring at the ceiling. Sometimes I hear the creaks of doors and footsteps up above. I try to ignore and fall asleep, but then the trumpet player starts. Peace is a wonderful thing.

NOVEMBER 14th

Strolling down Via Oberdan making for my flat, I spot him - a man sitting in a silent black car. He's watching a portone and I see him glance at his watch. The engine's off. He gives off a vibe – a scary one. Dressed in dark attire, he sits there quietly watching and waiting, all snake, and when I pop out later to the shop, he's still there. This time he's not alone. Two men sit zitta watching the portone. Silent. The morning street is alive but subdued,shopkeepers do their thing. I try not to look but do so from one corner of my eye. I look down from my balcony a few moments after, shaded by a curtain. They can't see me but are still there . The next time I look, they've gone. And so you could presume many things. The pragmatic would say, waiting for a friend, but it wasn't this, I'm sure. Perhaps detectives on a case, or else.

I hear the rumblings of a motorbike from down the road, on Viale Japigia.

As I lie on my siesta bed, I think about the watching, waiting car; its darkened tones and then recall the number plate. No number plate at all. That's what had struck as strange and made it odd. That and the silent, watching men.

So as I leave my flat that sunny afternoon for my afternoon lessons, I'm relieved to just see a loving mamma with two sweet kids; a cute dog and the guard. I don't see any bin lifters, bird-like ladies, Harbs or else. Just the normal occurrences of a small town in southern Italy. Nothing of any consequence.

NOVEMBER 15th

A beautiful November day and I don't hear the strange birdie sounds or the shouty neighbours. I'm thankful for the latter. Here we are still enjoying the sunkissed streets and there is only a slight nip in the air. The evenings are cooler but compared to northern parts, seem positively tropical. And so I walk the streets with sunglasses welded permanently to my forehead. I've been a sunglasses lover as far back as I recall .Perhaps, if truth be told, they form a shield from prying eyes and give a sense of privacy, something I feel lacks in our modern world, with the internet and all that jazz.

Oh for the past!

And so I think of England from years before these modern times, and how we used to live. I remember traipsing to the red boxes to make a call then, picking up the handset to discover there's no line. Reversing the charges to parents and popping in a 2p coin, the boxes invariably smelt of pee and other offensive things, and then, in winter, a broken pane here or there, would ensure maximum discomfort.

And now we have the mobile phone.

Not far from the school, near the post office, there is a place which translates as phone hospital with its regular queue for Dr. Phone, to cure all ailments. One day, I entered as my battery was running low. The phone's,that is. However, they had none and so I spent two hours scavenging the town for a replacement. I like that Zen thing of simplification, and yet life seems ever more cluttered. Even in Italy, you do the rounds of mundanity; the roaming charge extortionate and all that stuff.

So sometimes I like to find a space, away from all modernity, just to be. And rest.

Mindfulness I think they call it.

My favourite is a church where I can sit and reflect, away from mundane concerns.

 I think about my early life spent there each and every Sunday morn, and the Girl Guides and Sunday School, seemingly at crack of dawn. I'd carry a tiny 6d in my hand, back in the '60s and be in my Sunday best, and then we'd go on some trip afterwards to a beautiful part of northern England, like Silverdale or the Lakes.

Every time I entered the church, I'd be struck by the altar piece with ten commandments clearly written above stained glass windows; the lectern where the sermons were read and the vicar's robes. I'd also notice the flowers and where people sat. Often it would be the same place every week; all creatures of habit. Occasionally a newcomer would alter this equilibrium and all would feel awry a moment, yet would default the next time..

And once, some years ago, I stood in Siena's cathedral and looked up at the lofty ceiling. The stunning building, majestic and striped on the outside and ornate inside. For all its beauty and architecture, the thing that struck the most was the ambience. It was, to be simplistic, truly peaceful and seemed the epitome of all things sacred. I'd go there in troubled times and feel it washing over me – all right and sanctuary.

And so today, I walk to the Duomo, mobile off. I don't want to connect with the everyday world at all, but with higher things. I see a thousand teenagers busy texting he or she, then bypass the glam shops and their consumer goods. I wander by the profit banks, the tourist shops and tat and look upon the street vendors with gentle sympathy. I haven't yet arrived but feel already there, and when I enter the large building, I sense a cooling air.

It's November, Lecce is alive, and yet there is always space for other dimensions. So I sit awhile, and think about the sense of greatness and purity. Switching off from the modern world, I shake off my petty concerns then glance around me at the walls and altar space before.

It seems to cure me of my ailment – let's call it modern life - and so refreshed I feel able to proceed, a little lighter and less burdened with it all.

Yet only two minutes outside, there sits a young beggar on his own and it makes me wonder why. He looks genuine so I pass him some coins which he places carefully in a hat. I doubt he's really on his own but he gives an impression of utter isolation.

I reflect how it will be for him in the winter months, when even the sunbathed streets of Lecce will have their moments of chill and wonder if he ever thinks of higher things or maybe he doesn't have the privilege of time to spare, so focused on survival.

If I have learnt anything in this long and windy life, it's that life isn't fair and that's hard to accept.

Meandering back along the streets, which are quite busy now, laughter abounds and voices reach out. I smile a while at this snapshot of life and wonder how the south of Italy was a thousand years ago, maybe two. How was the south of Italy then? I conclude that some things may have been the same – the yearning for higher things and the dashing of hopes. Perhaps you can't assume that it was better or worse. Perhaps it just depended on your point of view.

NOVEMBER 18th

Sitting in the corner cafe, glasses askew and bag hugged beside me, I pick up a copy of 'Il quotidiano di Lecce'. Looking at the mug shots on the front page, I feel a little uneasy. It is disconcerting sometimes to be in such an attractive place, so at odds with the darkness of crime. I sometimes see things I'm worried about and wonder what is really going on, but I never ask. I ll never ask. Plump tanned hands appear with my morning elixir of happiness, and I flick through the pages with a curious eye. The skies are a little leaden today, so I take my street vendor's umbrella with me as I meander the Leccese streets towards Piazza Mazzini. There are a number of workers waiting to be picked up, I'm guessing to work at a factory or on a farm. They are all wearing red caps and look resigned. It's nearly 10 o'clock and I'm meeting my friend Maria for a chat. A slow pace turns brisk as I reach Piazza Sant'Oronzo, and smile at the little dogs yapping around the place. Some teenagers are hanging outside McDonald's, trying to look mean, as they often do. A bunch of taxi drivers are chatting outside their cabs, banter flowing, faces jovial, and carabinieri wander about the place in their cars, looking every inch the cool of Italy.

Maria, there by a pillar, looks radiant and friendly as I approach. It's good to see her and we gabble to one another about this and that, life and the universe. Arriving at the Duomo cafe, we order drinks then recline into comfy seats, surrounded by the papers. I point to the mugshots on today's papers, and Maria laughs with abandonment, not giving care to such negativities. It is one of the things I love about Italians -they are upbeat and positive, refusing to let life's dark moments intrude too much on inner joy. There are grave problems in Italy, but no one cares about it, on the surface, and so they smile and joke instead. That's not to say they're negligent about the country's woes. Far from it. Of course, they care deep down about the injustices, the criminality, the petty crime, the financial crisis – it's just that they have positive thinking in the bag and refuse point blank to focus on it. I admire this quality and wish to be more like them. You will notice that if you try to swing the conversation towards such negativities, for the most part, it will be quickly dismissed to far sunnier topics. Italians seem to love the summer as much as we do. They often talk about their holidays and the best places to go. They love the whole thing, from May to November – the basking in it and the lure of the seas. I am almost surprised by this. After all, you'd think they'd tire of it, given the abundance of summery weather here, but they positively revel in it, rejecting all signs of winter. Any mention of the W word is met with a grimace and slight frown although trips to ski slopes will engender much enthusiasm. The crazy guy is wandering about again, muttering to himself. I feel sorry, but have a healthy dose of caution around him. The unpredictable nature is what one fears the most. How sad. To be in such a beautiful place, but so 'elsewhere'. Noone pays him the slightest regard. He shouts and sings and mutters, but it is as if he doesn't exist. A ghostly figure on the steps of the cathedral. At times he reminds me of a football fan, with his chants and songs, but then I see the madness in his eyes and realise, it's another type of tournament altogether.

Maria tells me about her two sons. I can see how proud she is and I understand, as I am also so proud of my own. She tells me a little of her life, and I enjoy her tales of childhood and youth and how her life has been so different to my own, and yet so similar. We decide to walk a while and so wander to the grand 16th century Porta Napoli before a slow approach to the beautiful buildings and shops of the centre. It's beginning to rain and I

pop up my street vendor brolly with its red tartan pattern. It's a little chilly, but nothing a jumper can't fix. Hungry I head for a shop with Maria to buy bread, formaggio, olives and some plump health -giving fruit. Laden with the goods I wander back to my flat – past the small dogs and their pets, those big strong men; the besuited males rushing to some business meeting or other; the Baroque buildings; the plush shops and the homeless beggars. One lunges suddenly towards me, and for a split second I think that I'm about to be attacked. All my defences are up; that which makes us animals to the fore. However, the poor soul had just tripped on an upturned paving stone, with no malice intended at all. The pavements do leave something to be desired; great gaping holes and uneven footing a daily hazard for the unwary. I sometimes feel that I am about to fall into another place. I try not to care and I keep one eye on the street and one on the ground at all times. I also keep a third on the traffic. I've just spotted Signora Caparcio and she's waving to me. I like that. It makes me feel more at home and comfortable with the whole thing. On the wall of the newsagents, there's an old-fashioned cigarette machine. In spite of the obvious health associations, I warm to the image with its connotations of better (unhealthier) times. The little drawers and buttons enthral me and remind me of my childhood when bubble gum machines and callipered charity boxes stood patiently outside English shops. I remember the corner sweet shop near to my house, and the jars of multi-coloured sweeties just waiting to be poured into small, greasy white paper bags for greedy little hands. I remember pear drops and blackcurrant lollies. Even toffee lollies. I remember my first pet cat Toffee. A wistful sadness takes over me, but I walk back to the flat with the next step of my journey.

NOVEMBER 20th

Sitting in the upmarket corner patisserie; the glamorous one with its sweetmeats bounty I sit awhile to drink a cappuccino, opposite the kitchen where the deliciousness is made and I watch as they scurry like groomed mice around the room. A powerful memory grips me.

I remember my first cook book with its bright illustrations. A large thing. Colourful. Lollipops and ice-cream; fairy cakes and tat. Then I recall at school, making rock buns that indeed justified the name.

Our strict teacher wasn't impressed.

Placed in a basket with patterned cover, I collected them after school all tinned and for the table. Not good for the teeth but quite good to the taste. All currant and sugar and bite. Not bad, the first time. They got eaten. The proof was in. Then the most delicious thing - a meringue affair with pineapple custard. A roux. The taste divine. Buttery too. And speaking of which, a Bread & Butter pudding. The marmalade slices all upright like soldiers then paired with the eggy cream, turned into something gorgeous after the oven. It must have worked as I made it often. And suet pud stodgy and laboured or Queen of Puddings, all jammy and light. Not quite. Cooking lessons were not a joy because of the teacher we had. All bark and bite and little pleasure. I remember the arched eyebrows and starched apron. How we toiled, all sweaty and perturbed.

But later on, at home, I'd fiddle and potter with this taste or that and create nice puds. Edible even, and enjoyable. I always liked licking the bowl when my mother made cakes. She was the cake baker supreme. They always turned out well – the tiered ones; the Victorias; the birthday s and the Butterflys. Her birthdays were the best. All chocolate and cocoa buttercream yet bouncy and light. Divine. And her jam tarts. Exquisite.

The sweet gloop of a rice pudding made with love and splodged with treacle. And then to sit and watch 'Man about the House' or 'The Saint'; all cosy in the nest. Early '70s.

I look at the shop's cakes; the Zeppole and tarts; the glazed strawberries and fruity ones in satisfying shapes and then the boxes for their transportation. Square and white and clean. The scoops and tongs and custard ones; a sweet toother's dream.

But I love the savoury too. And so the Cheese Cauliflower and home-made curry would bubble on the stove then sit whilst watching Corrie, being eaten. Yum. My mother loved Fruit Squares and I the orange ones - a treat sometimes and flaked with coconut.

And back further into time, the Snowball – the coconut capped things or mother's Shepherd's pie. Her Chicken Fricassee all comfort food, for cold wintery days; that and Scrabble, Cocoa and Gilberto O'Sullivan. Heaven early '70s. The Carpenters playing softly in the wings. All divine. Homely. Just home.

NOVEMBER 22nd

Barletta. A place of great personal importance. I once lived there back in 1989. It opened a door and several windows; perhaps a mansion.

Incredible as it is, there is still a warmth in the air and I am yet to don my winter wear. It is with this abandonment that I set off for a weekend there. I already booked my precious ticket on 'La Freccia Bianca' and amble my way to Lecce train station in great anticipation. I am expecting delays and disappointments, but this expectation is about to be dashed as my train arrives early. I smile at the irony and sit beside a black clad old lady with a story to tell. Her ruddy wrinkled complexion masks a sad wisdom – a lady who has travelled far. An old man sits beside us, newspaper in hand and tut on his lips. He doesn't approve of this world and expresses this without a word. I did return recently, after some 23 years. Interesting. Some naughty children play nearby, a sweet reminder of better times and days, when the world was more simple somehow – at least through the perspective of my rose tinted glasses. The train arrives – the end of the line with only one direction to follow. This one is heading for Turin and some of the passengers seem bound for there, although it has many stops en route. I find my seat and observe all the peculiarities of the carriage. Its drink holder and folding table; its wi-fi socket and intercom. It's soothing somehow, this train. The passengers are noisy in an unthreatening way, nice but noisy. They enjoy their trip. They enjoy their lives. They know how to live, Italians.

They understand the journey is short, but to be enjoyed. The views are magnificent, of olive groves and yellow flowers; of autumn colours and faded palazzi. The blue sea beyond, shimmering like glass. We journey on, through the major towns of Brindisi and Bari, the backstreet stations, the less pleasant parts. Passengers embark and disembark, clutching bags closely to themselves. A student or two look lost. The train continues through Giovinazzo with its green-shuttered turret and Trani with its three tiered cathedral. This is train candy. This is it. This is what it's all about. This. Arriving in Barletta, is chaotic. People everywhere, nice or not, of every type and persuasion. I hustle through to the exit steps and find my friends waiting, like a warm cup of tea on a winter's day then we wander past giant bronze Eraclio as if this is a normal thing. Gargantuan and impressive he looms over everyone by the old town with its quaint limestoned streets and gay shop awnings. A cappuccino or two by the Duomo then to St. Patrick's. A delicious meal and some

lovely company. I love this town and the people, so full of brio. It is a fleeting visit though and I must return tomorrow, so I repair onward to my place and sanctuary for the night. Sleep. By tomorrow I will have returned to Lecce. And so the dawn sees me teetering on Barletta's train platform where the weird and the wonderful strut around like some strange surreal dream – the well-dressed businessmen are weaved by homeless beggars and drug addicts. A man is bin picking which reminds me of Lecce. My train arrives on time and I'm not disappointed...

NOVEMBER 25th

I do believe the weather is starting to turn. A slight cool breeze rustles my neighbours' sheets on her balcony; an irony as they assured me it never gets cold here. I'm starting to think of hats and gloves, so decide to head for Benetton. What a rainbow of colours awaits. I spy a small plum hat with matching gloves and make it my own. I am glad of them that evening at the school, when it gets even colder. My students are poised but also share my discomfort, so I sit with coat on, whilst I teach, then jump around madly between lessons to warm up.

A quick whizz to the corner bar and an Espresso, warms me up sufficiently, but also gives me

insomnia later on. My teenagers are as sharp as razors today, whilst my brain on a go-slow.

I wander back after work and spot a tiny mottled grey kitten miaowing anxiously near a bush.

There is no sight of its mother and my heart goes out to it. It also gives me the dilemma of

how to help. Luckily, a kind woman and her daughter arrive and look after it. They are good people, I feel instinctively, so I feel able to leave kitty in their hands. A street vendor

approaches me with sad eyes. I can't resist and hand him two Euros even though I'm running low myself. I don't take any of his goods in exchange. He is very grateful, as if his life depended on it.

Maybe it did. I see some merry friends outside a cafe bar. Laughing. Joking. Carefree. There is an insular inclusion to their lives – you're either in, or you're very much out. The strange man is wandering about again. I avoid eye contact. The hairdressers are smoking outside their shop. It's ok. I feel fine. A sense of calm descends on me. A friendly neighbour greets me, 'Ciao!' I feel I'm being included.

Feeling a little more weary than usual, I wander towards the school – across the six-laned road and the near death experience; the supermercato then the old ladies at the launderette who wave as cheerily as ever when I pass. I feel my wave is a little more feeble this morning, the brain less alert. Soon I am ensconced in a lesson with all my will to stay alert and on top of things. My students are perceptive and realise I am tired. They smile benevolently, and marvel at my confusions whilst accepting my 'moments' of ineptitude. A

sad light ensues as I head towards Viale Japigia. It seems so wrong to have the leaden clouds that hang pregnantly over the city. My layers are slowly building to a crescendo and the bank guard looks a little cold. I am ready for some lunch and a siesta, but when I open my apartment door, I find a lot of people in the kitchen. This is torture, there upon my tiredness, so I make my excuses and climb into bed. Waking only fractionally before work re-starts, I make a momentous decision to have a real Cappuccino.

Oh joy to feel the pulse a-racing and the excited sense of being in the picture and not on the edges.

Brimming with renewed enthusiasm, I rush to lessons and enjoy every minute of them, throwing with gusto the complexities of Phrasal Verbs and the Present Perfect tense. Only little Mario subdues my spirits a moment, when he reflects upon the stupidity of the English language. He pouts before continuing his stubborn pursuit of his favourite toys.

My student friend Maria offers me a lift back and I readily accept. We have a great chat in those five minutes – me in my Italian, she in her newly acquired smattering of English. She tells me about her cousin's cafe in the centre of town, so doubtless another coffee call.

We say goodbye, and I wander towards the great portone and wait like a statue whilst a large

family finish their conversation in the doorway.

Climbing the five flights of stairs, a head quickly scurries back into its flat and a loud female voice can be heard admonishing, or maybe just talking with, an enfeebled husband. My flatmates are in and so we sit and chat a while whilst making some food. Daniella tells me how she has fallen in love with Lecce and has always liked the place. She restores Art so I can imagine this is true. It would be hard not to love Lecce if you were in any way connected with art or architecture. I have fallen in love with Baroque. I am amazed at the intricacies, the decoration, the time that was spent on each inch of the buildings here. I don't think I've fallen in love with Lecce though. Lecce has a claustrophobic air, in the suburbs, mainly due to its relentless buildings. I can feel hemmed in here and this isn't something I like to feel. I'm beginning to long for wide open spaces, some greenery, perhaps some sea. I'm beginning to want to travel around more. Maybe, in a small way I'm missing England. I certainly miss my son, my husband and my cat, but England is a strange one. I don't miss England at all when I'm in Italy. Che strano!

Climbing into bed, I ponder all these things and more, and as if by magic, I fall asleep, nonostante the caffeine...

CHAPTER THREE - DECEMBER

DECEMBER 1st

It's cooler today but there is still a hint of the summer in the air. I wake up to the aroma of freshly brewed coffee which wafts from the kitchen into my room and prepares me for the day. My flat-mate enters the kitchen to gather her things as she's leaving for Rome today. She looks a little stressed. Perhaps it is the train journey, or other things ... As she leaves, she looks back at me sadly and I can tell she is upset about something. She'll be back next week, she says. Her hand trembling , I feel sorry as she leaves the flat, all burdened with a case. She's proud and I know not to ask. I gather up my laundry from the balcony and put it on the bed. Still a little damp from the increasingly humid air, a small dog barks. I can tell from the tone that it's a small beast – a small lamenting pet. It even sounds distressed. I tell myself its owners are out at work, and that is its complaint. I can't bear to think otherwise.

A weaker sun glows in the distance on bejumpered souls rushing hither and thither. The cars are racing steadily to their goal, but maybe the goal posts will shift. Life is like that.

Today I have a lot to do. Five classes and some. As I approach the school, I see the man outside the supermarket pretending to be lame, with a cap to his side. I am not cynical, but I have seen him walking at a brisk pace near my flat. I ignore him.

However, another genuine, so I drop a coin or two in his palm. He looks too young and it saddens me. What happened to him? What is his story?

My class are there before me today and sit patiently awaiting some revelation of knowledge. It's not forthcoming but I try. We're doing food vocabulary, and so I set up a mock cafe and restaurant scenario. As is so often the case with my lessons, it turns into a comedy show, and tears are literally streaming down my face. I try hard to be professional, but when you are with people of similar humour, all masters in the art of self- mockery, you're in trouble. As the students confuse their foods with their requests, I sit there awhile and observe them. Italian faces are wonderful - often good-looking but always full of expression and character. Their eyes and hands tell me how much they're enjoying themselves and that makes me feel good in turn.

It's brightened up as I leave the school – but still everyone looks scuppered. We all have that in mind.

The laundry ladies told me it never gets cold, but I'm not so sure. Everyone is wrapped up now in their layers so hardly the stuff of eternal summer. The street beggars are still there. I

enter the supermarket to buy some Pecorino and pane. The olives are looking inviting today, so I ask one scoop, and no more. Once in the shop, it is hard to leave. The vegetable assistant is inundated on a daily basis and, although we all wait patiently, underneath my toe is tapping. Then, there's the chatty old man who likes to pass the time of day and an exhausting wait at the Delicatessen counter. To get to the exit, is blessed relief until the fake beggar looks up appealingly at you. He is definitely better off than me, but I am tired and not up to being callous. I drop a coin in his hat and walk on by. The post office queue is getting longer and Italians are not quiet about their displeasures. They have plenty of suggestions on offer and all claim their priority.

I return to my empty flat and feel a little sad. There's a dull ache in me that has arrived almost from nowhere. I don't feel too good so I lunch, then take a short siesta before the next onslaught of lessonry. It's 2.30pm and I can hear a baby crying, a dog barking and a man snoring. I make myself a tea, eager to taste a little of home. The thought

becomes compelling, 'What am I doing here? Why did I come?' I can't answer that right now.

Soon I am walking back to the school, swinging my bag and waving to the bank guard, avoiding the ever impending threat of a traffic death, working through my next lesson in my head. I approach the bar opposite the school and rejoice. The big fat corner chair is empty. I like that. I can sit and read the papers before school. A crazy guy wanders past the bar and makes me nervous, but the newspaper headlines, even more so. It's strange to live in a beautiful world, where ugly things go virtually unnoticed. I admire the adept manner of the barmaid at dealing with the unsavoury. She avoids eye contact and carries on. So do I. I wave to an early arriver at the school and finish the article I'm reading. The paper is practically gobbled up by someone nearby. It is something that we hunger for here. News. Bella figura only goes so far.

DECEMBER 2nd

I do recall thinking some months ago that one of the greatest pleasures in being down here in Lecce was the sense of eternal summer but the days are rather cool now. It still surprises me to don a woollen hat and mitts even though logic tells me it can't be eternal summer anywhere. The avoidance of an icy street is a small compensation, however, and evenings more in the balance, without their shedding of light. As I meander slowly towards the school, I decide to pop into the stationery shop en route to see if they have glitters for the kids. The shelves pile high like a wedding cake, with colours on every corner. I have to always remember not to touch stuff, a habit I'm used to in England, as it is not the done thing here. However, I'm longing to pick up the notebooks and pads to see how they differ and examine the colours in more detail. This requires not only gaining the assistant's attention, but waiting patiently for them to get said things off the high shelves with the use of a ladder. As they are clearly busy this morning, I tell them I'll pop back shortly and wander further towards the school. This is just before bumping into my ancient admirer Ernesto who decides I should be chaperoned the twenty yards to the school. The passage is a little tense as I'm hardly in the mood for chat, but it isn't easy to brush off the offers of gifts and cappuccinos that are somehow squeezed into a small space of pavement. The pavement is a pleasing grid pattern that reminds me of my old swimming pool in Lancaster. The pool was neatly tiled and heavily chlorinated. No wonder we gasped as we entered, after dutifully plopping our feet into disinfected waters. My main memories of the time relates to the subdued temperature. The water, the changing rooms and the wait outside for a lift were invariably cold and only warmed by a plastic cup of '60s cocoa from a whirring drinks machine. I enter the school to see the secretary busy at computer and teachers ensconced in their respective rooms and then I remember my mission for the stationery. This is a game of dodgems as I attempt to avoid my ancient admirer and the 'bin lifter' as well as the ubiquitous 'He s alright really but he killed a few people some years ago' one, HARB for brevity as aforementioned

Arriving at the Stationers, I'm pleased to see a bit of space in the shop (a somewhat rare moment in Italy) and at least the possibility of some assistance from the harrassed looking woman. She precariously climbs the ladder to obtain the books that I require, and wraps them neatly in paper. So much for checking that they are what I need, I submit to my destiny. A few glittery pens later and some more coloured paper sees me heading to the school. Unfortunately they only had gold and silver that day so young Mario tells me, in no uncertain terms, that it's simply not good enough as he wants red. Not only this, but he cries hysterically at the misfortune and I take a few deep breaths of contrition.

Another memory comes to me from my early school days. I recall the experience of colouring in Christmas cards with crayons, to take home to some hapless parents. How we longed for the crayons to be complete and new, instead of the short stubby monstrosities we had to bear with. It was an indignity as you tried to colour in an angel's hair with the stumped yellow, for it to break up in your fingers. This indignity would sometimes be followed by Recorder practice. Although I loved music, the Recorder could have put paid to that for life.

'Little Bird' became an over familiar feature of my young life, and one I can't forget.

And, to think back then I had no knowledge of Babbo Natale; only that big red clad man called Santa Claus who I hoped would be benevolent enough each year to gift me what I wanted.

So, for example, there was the Tiny Tears phase. How I wanted one. Oh my! And it could wee too which became the secret of its success. Not only this, but you fed it to produce such a skill. When I was lucky enough to receive one at Christmas, Santa became my new best friend. Now all I needed was a pair of plastic shoes to go with. How I longed for these. It's funny how small things can become huge as a child. I remember the moment we found some, in some hillbilly shop on the Yorkshire moors. They smelt of 1960s plastic and were pale pink in colour, but they fit. Oh boy!

I wish I could make Mario a little happier.

He really is upset with the red glitter situation. I suppose we were never entirely content with Etch-a-Sketch either.

So the Christmas spirit is alive and well!

DECEMBER 5th

A cat is miaowing on the balcony opposite and I can see two pert ears between the plant pots by the old boiler that is huffing and puffing away. Soon I'll be returning home for Christmas

and I have become so used to my life here now that it seems implausible to be back in the Lancastrian streets, at the supermarket or hearing the local accent on the bus. My flight booked, I'm beginning to look forward to it, although I have much to do until that time. My lessons beckon and today sees the teenagers at their best. They are excited about Christmas and the small ones even more. There is a sense of festivities to come in the streets and shop windows.

Everyone looks more excitable in the changing light, the shops a little fuller.

The lesson with my small children is a riot, though in a good way. They are beside themselves in anticipation of Babbo Natale. One of them has even brought a toy version and finds it very much in demand. Tiny children pull at the poor toy's arms and legs until it cascades to the floor and gets forgotten, but for its jolly song which rumbles on beneath the desk.

The evening dark draws in early and I observe the two fat pigeons opposite the school. They huddle together for warmth and seem less playful. As I hurry back to my flat, I have three thoughts in mind - eat, bathe and sleep. It has been a long day.

DECEMBER 10th

Now it is really cold and I am struggling to keep warm at night. I have taken to wearing a deeply unsexy woollen hat in bed as well as the lifesaving hot water bottle which I only managed to acquire through the kindness of a colleague. I hug it until it can be hugged no more, and it has become my confidante through the lonely hours. Sometimes, I do feel lonely here, without much sense of a home and the couple below argue continually, making for an uncomfortable atmosphere. It's only in the golden light of morning that I feel alive and happy again, with the irrepressible spirit of Italy, always brighter than our own, so you can't help but be lifted from the glooms

The day runs smoothly and is helped along by delicious seafood pasta lunch and a Funghi supper. To say I have lived in food heaven today would be an understatement. Sometimes just the simple pleasure of eating here in Italy, makes life worth living and everything better – even perfect. Perfection is maybe deluded, but as reality is how we perceive things, then my reality is at times perfect.

DECEMBER 11th

They're there again. That couple. The moon is full tonight but dark corners loom in all directions. Arriving back at my flat gate, I fumble for the keys. Uneasy as a drunken gang shuffle nearby, it's quite a walk from gate to door, through lurking shadows. The car sits quietly, purring. I see heads bowed. A furtive kiss. A glance at a watch. A man looks through his window. He leans out. About 30. He's watching the scene. I fumble again nervously for my keys and drop them in the inky black, the satisfying click of the lock opening then closed. And so I shut out the couple and the leaning man. A light comes on. A timer. Soon it will snaffle out again as I reach the stairs. Someone comes out of the lift. I don't recognize him. He stares then rushes out. He and the couple and the leaning man and all. I'm on heightened senses. If I were a cat, my hair would be right up. A creepy vibe. And then the lights go. I reach for a switch . Illuminated once more. Third floor. Nearly there. Now the fifth. I click the locks, twice to the left and open the door. It's pitch, until I find the light. Hearing footsteps on the stairs, I shut the door. Tight. I'm frightening myself. There is no reason but the moon and the blackness; a vague sense of foreboding. It's quiet now. All quiet. Too quiet. Acclimatized. I hear snoring from next door. The couple are asleep and so I soothe the room with soft lights and scented candles, have a bath and begin to relax until I hear the screeching of tyres fast into the night. All shut out. At least. Sleep.

DECEMBER 12th

There are some stairs at the end of my floor. They lead up to a door. It's always locked. No sound. But one evening in the gloom, I swear I saw someone turn the corner and up them. I looked but saw noone or nothing. I know it's not inhabited so what of it: Italy and its ghosts and ghouls.

Not only this but the exquisite.

Take Giovinazzo.

We holidayed there once.

An old man waved from the landmark green-shuttered turret. Ancient they were – both turret and man. Waving. Real. Not a ghost. We waved back. He told us of the sea and his fisherman tales. He'd been one years ago, before the sea defences came. Then the storms would whip up waves that reached his window, he said. He lived near the top. We'd had a pleasant afternoon and so had some kittens perched atop a boat. They'd enjoyed the fishy titbits and the lulling sun there all entwined on a boat. We liked Giovinazzo; a charming little town when we stayed nearby, with a beach to ourselves - our own treasure island, complete with old pier and swimming Bream. The only time marker, a large cruise ship rolling by. We forgot ourselves. Almost. And then the evenings graced us with pines and pink skies and gentle breezes. Giovinazzo. We liked very much. The exquisite.

So strange to be in an isolated outpost that is near the airport.

DECEMBER 15th

Walking along Viale Japigia; a slight nip to the air, I'm glad of my extra layers as I stroll uneven paving stones. The children, all wrapped up, look happy enough as they head for their schools. It's only 8.30 but I already feel a little weary. Perhaps I'm ready for my break. The thought of endless flights and all the waiting at airports puts me off, but I know I will enjoy it once I'm there. After a Cappuccino, I head back to the flat to quickly pack. Nothing overly taxing, but the basics. I'll probably get most of my Christmas presents at the airport, though the guilty thought of English ones seems quite beguiling.

I compile a small list: Coffee, chocolates, that sort of thing. A few tubes of Baci always go down well.

I'm out again and having a peep through the gift shop window. I don't see anything that grabs me. Then, suddenly, as if I'd pressed the wrong button, up pops Ernesto. He's walking as a fast as he can from the corner bar in my direction.

'Ma Signora,' he says with a faux expression of guilessness,'Sei qui'.

Yes Ernesto I'm here, I reply, and searching for Christmas presents.

'Let me buy you one' he says in Italian.

'No thanks' I reply, 'There's really no need'.

This has distracted me from the time and I suddenly realise that I'm forgetting morning lessons! With a cheery wave, I try to cross the six-laned road as quickly as humanly possible to grab my books, then about turn in the direction of the school. When I arrive, I'm not late but neither am I as early as is comfortable. I have lesson prep to do. And who is waiting there by the entrance?

Ernesto of course. Looking a little sheepish, but nonetheless happy, he hands me a gift wrapped box.

'All women like chocolates', he croons. I can hardly argue so quickly thank him and rush into the school.

'Ooh!' My students tease. 'A present? Is it your birthday?'

'No' I reply, 'Just a Christmas present.'

'Lovely.' They reply. And then, as if I'd waved a magic wand, out come theirs. Each and every one had bought me something. I was truly touched.

Needless to say, I knew I'd be busy in that gift shop the following day reciprocating the thought.

Later that evening, between lessons, I head for the corner cafe and down an Espresso. So tired, even if I know it will keep me semi awake. There he is again. Ernesto.

He asks me if I've eaten them yet and that I'm not to eat them till Christmas day then think of him'

I feel a little guilty and embarrassed. Ok, I smile.

The evening seems endless . The walk back to my flat all lead weight and some. The six-laned road, even at 9 of the evening is busy. Perhaps they too are doing their Christmas duties.

I wander along uneven stones. It's quite dark now and I feel a little nervous until I reach my palazzo.

The couple are sitting in a car down a small side street. Perhaps there is something illicit about them. Maybe an affair. She is glamorous and he looks nervously through the car window.

I hear the yapping of the Leccese dogs. They seem to know things are afoot. So when I reach Via Oberdan, I rush a little to the great portone, past a group of maleducati, and through the door. Clanked shut I feel relieved. I look across the road and see my landlord's shop. Someone is still there working. The hallway is dark as I start to climb the five long flights. Reaching the flat, I open my door to a warmth and cosy that really means something to me. Clicking the gas lighter, I make a Redbush tea and sit awhile recovering in the kitchen. I notice how cold my fingertips are and breathe on them. A little late.

In my room there's still packing to be done, but the couple below are arguing which sets my nerves on edge. Sometimes it sounds as if they're about to kill each other. I put in my earplugs and do a bit of packing.

Outside, down in the street, loud voices echo. Again there is something menacing. I focus on the break. Now I'm looking forward, in spite of the long journey.

I lie on my bed thinking of all I have to do. Making a list is imperative. Without them I'm lost. I feel listless. Tired. So tired. I fall asleep fully clothed.

DECEMBER 20th

It is the last day of term. Exhausted I have a long journey before me, but I'm so looking forward to seeing my beloved family. As is always the case when you are looking forward to something, every second becomes an hour; an hour a week. Will the day ever end I wonder and will tomorrow follow?

My final lessons are a sweet melee of Christmas greetings and jovial good will. We laugh and sing; smile and joke.

Everyone seems ready for a good long break. My three little girls are happy with their chocolate gifts, bought from the nearby shop. A joy to teach, they're not only bright but also respectful and nice. I don't remember this from my English state school days!

Returning to my flat I finish packing for the long day ahead. I'm to

be at Brindisi airport by 10 am so order a taxi. They're pretty good

round here. Reliable. I'm not a good flier so nerves begin to set in.

I can't imagine how I'll cope with the long hours ahead. I have three

flights in front of me and this is difficult to swallow for someone

scared of it.

DECEMBER 21st

Sitting in the back of my airport taxi, wedged in by my case, we wend our way along the

motorway, with worrying cars whizzing by and beautiful olive groves gracing the airport-

bound journey.

I wonder how the day will unfold and answer the taxi driver's questions about my entire

life. The peach-toned palazzi and postered walls fly by. An odd palm waves its fronds.

We nearly crash a few times, but that seems normal so when it starts to leave the racing

cars and heads through quiet country roads towards the airport, I realise that I'm on my

way home.

It's a beautiful sunny day, in spite of the date, and I look up at the skies and wonder about

the leaden ones to come.

When I arrive at Brindisi airport, the place is packed with those heading this place or that.

Near the cafe I see Lecce's mayor who's apparently on his travels. I pass on by to be

respectful then at the gate, I sit with an elderly woman. She's an academic flying up to

Milan to see her son and very nervous about the flight so I try to reassure her, but then so

am I. It's a windy day. We chat nervously about nothing and everything until our time.

As I walk across the tarmac to the plane, I have that thought ; the one I always have these days. Perhaps this will be my time. I try to be philosophical . Che sera sera. The old lady treads nervously up the steps. I feel uneasy. It's quite windy today. The nerves are kicking in. I try not to let it overtake my emotions and focus instead on home. I pray a little then I smile. If this is it, I've had a good innings, I reflect, then take my seat and await my fate.

Survived and deposited at Rome's Fiumicino, perhaps a little rattled and rolled, it's fortunate that I see a plethora of desired items here, once suctioned through the controls. I nearly buy the shop of calendars and scarves, although there is admittedly one downside to this – each has a distinctly Roman theme which is hardly fitting. The black leather belt I bought from a street vendor looked nice at the time, but the thought of black market goods for your Christmas present doesn't appeal, so that got stuffed in the bin. The array of handbags on Via Trinchese looked the job too but were hardly Italian. Needless to say most had arrived from China and other parts. No worries. The Leccese tourist guide books look attractive enough to gift, so a couple of them along with the calendars, all displaying the Oronzo statue, will suffice.

I also buy Baci chocolates of course, all in slim tubes, but have to admit that there was one less by the time I arrived back in Manchester some three flights later...

CHAPTER FOUR – JANUARY

JANUARY 8th

After three weeks of leaden sky, it's good to be heading back to better climes, sad though I am as I wait for the train at Lancaster station and wave goodbye to my husband, the dull sky overhead. It was hard to say goodbye to my son the day before; every time breaks my heart. As I journey to Manchester, I watch the fields and town houses whizz by, and see the sleepy faces transfixed by their mobiles and gadgets; or lost in a book. It's really cold and I'm wearing several layers though I know I will regret later on, when I sit in some overheated airport lounge or other, gasping for cool.

Checking in sees me soon boarding my flight to Paris Charles de Gaulle airport, with barely any time until my next to Milan. I stuff a ghastly chocolate chip cookie in my mouth and speak Frenglit in my total confusions, forgetting even the most rudimentary French. Aboard my Milan bound flight sits a French businessman. He dusts off my tray for me and uprights my chair then gives me good advice whilst telling me of his travels to the far east. He's very nice, but in a business like way, without too much sentiment or fuss. By accident, I sit on his laptop as I try to leave the seat on arrival, but he's good humoured and gracious about it. I am thankful for this small mercy. Milan Linate airport seems small and compact, after Paris, and in its small enclosure lie several classy shops selling clothes and perfumes, sweetmeats and gifts. I ignore all but head for the busy cafe with endless queues to wait my turn for a Cappuccino. I always forget to pay first and get the ticket before asking for the drink, so this delays by a good ten minutes. Once achieved, I perch on a high seat, like a harried bird, and slurp my drink. My mobile battery needs recharging so I wait until I can contact my husband and son to let them know where I am. I have a couple of hours here and find myself moving every hour or so to a different waiting location, to avert the inevitable boredom. The hours go by so slowly as some song goes, until I see the steady arrival of people who are waiting for my flight to Brindisi. On board, I am wedged between a strange Austrian woman and a nervous Slovenian girl. They don't know each other at first, but by the end of the flight, seem to have known each other all their lives. This confuses me and I trust neither, which may or may not be justified. The plane rattles on ever more over the Appenines, dipping down uncomfortably here and there through turbulent skies.

I cannot believe when we touch down as it seemed an impossible journey, but I am soon being escorted to my flat by my boss. It isn't noticeably warmer than England, but I see it all with fresh eyes again – the palms, the olive groves, the villas and the graffitied signs -all foreign and interesting. It's dark by the time I get back to my flat. I have in my possession one very useful item – a bottle of milk, with the last of my tea bags still there in the cupboard, I make my first cup of tea on arrival.

Even the caffeine and the ensuing pasta are not enough to keep me awake. And so I sleep and sleep and sleep, until the next day.

JANUARY 9th

Ah January in Italy. It reminds me of the year I first went to Barletta first. 1989. I recall arriving at Fiumiciano airport, from Luton airport, to be greeted by new boss, John. A nice English fellow who had given up academia in the homeland for sunnier climes. He'd escorted me, via one creaky plane over the Appennines, to Bari airport from where I was taken by car to Barletta. It was Operation Mystery as it unfolded. And to think I'd nearly taken the TEFL job in Calabria teaching carabinieri. Now that would have been interesting! As it was, the months in Barletta proved a wonderful experience for a young woman, and my memories are mainly of sunny days and fun evenings. As time tends to dull the worst moments, I'll overlook the gun wielding robbers or the flat being emptied of its paltry goods as these seemed minor things at the time. What really mattered was bonding with the locals and improving the lingo. So here I am, some twenty five years on, perhaps too old for this game but doing the same things in another location. Superficially all seems similar - still the jaw dropping architecture, the delicious foods and the glamorous natives yet it couldn't be more different. Time has whitewashed the country. Time has white washed the world. Nothing is really the same. A peculiar sensation pervades. To think that this light is much as it was back in 1989. The pasta was still being served al dente and the glasses were still being filled with water and wine.Like a vacuum of consciousness, I feel as if I've been asleep for many years and now I'm waking up. It's a heady experience. I wave to Davide, the newsagent, as I pass by and reflect how this was much the same as I wandered towards the newsagent there, all those years ago. He was friendly too though in those days my Italian was less fluent. Sometimes you wonder if there is a way, somehow, of returning to your past, other than through memories. If only we could. Imagine the wonder and joy at seeing it again; all those moments that are gone but still with us.

JANUARY 10th

The lightening skies and fresh nip in the air are lovely after an English December. It's good to see my students again and I feel a new bond with them; that which comes after a prolonged period of seeing the same people twice a week. Even my wee ones seem glad to see me again. I load up with the coloured paper, pencils and glue from the local stationers before visiting my favourite supermercato for bread and cheese. I have a real problem deciding over the fragrant cheeses – should it be the speckled and gooey

Gorgonzola or the hard and holey Emmental, or should I be a bore and plump for my usual Stracchino? One thing's for sure – Stracchino is never boring.

I'm happy today as a friend is coming to see me after my classes, from Barletta. I've warned her that she'd better like cheese and she laughed at the thought.

My landlord's been in again and his wife has 'tidied up' for me. I do like a bit of privacy but have learned that I won't get it here.

The angry couple have been at it again so I had to warn my friend about that too. I told her to bring ear plugs just in case they're on a nocturnal one then popped into the deli opposite my flat to see the couple who run it. They are very friendly and although somewhat inflated pricewise, as informed by a street beggar the other day, I like to pop in for my milk and Artichokes, not to mention their Altamura panini. Everything they sell seems twice as delicious, though it might just be the patter. I also have a hair appointment with the flamboyant hairdresser on the corner. I know it will be a day of self-esteem bashing. Here they tell it like it is and my locks are a sorry sight to be sure. I am ready to take any insults they throw at me, and some. I like to remind myself that there's more to life than your wig, though it's harder to believe when you're in there than out!

I dash back to my flat for a chomp of cheese and a foily thing of Beatola whilst listening to the angry couple having a rant. Ear plugs in, and all is blissfully quiet, apart from the sound of my own jaws chomping on the food. I fall unexpectedly asleep whilst my curtain wafts and tufts of golden light filter through the shutters. My alarm does its job before I stroll to my classes, risking life and limb as usual on that six-laned road whilst waving to the friendly bank guard. My students are jolly today, which is pleasant after

the grumping that is

my shouty neighbours.

After work I pop down to my local bar to await my friend Anna. She's a little late and

I'm a little tired, but a glass of vino later and a 'putting the world to rights' chat sees me

perking up and even happy. Exhaustion evaporated, I'm reminded how good it is to be in

Italy again. It took a long time to return, but I'm glad I did.

JANUARY 11th

It's 5 am and I can hear a cat miaowing from some Leccese side street. I imagine the

Leccese cat to be super cool, glamorous and have a penchant for sweetened cream. The

cat is clearly wanting attention but the world is yet asleep and noone seems to hear, apart

from me.

Lazily, I wander into the kitchen to boil the small panned water for a tea, but alas there is

no water. No water at all. At first I think it must be my enfeebled twist of the tap, but

soon realise it to be a general problem. I don't even hear the common splashing of a

shower.

I've never been so keen to visit the corner bar as today, given the water situation, and so

it is with huge relish that I enjoy my first Cappuccio of the day, one of many. How many

times can a person visit a bar and not seem of unsound mind, I muse.

Of course this requires a rotation of sorts. A couple here, a couple there is all that's

necessary.

The bar staff must think they have exceptional service today and tire of waving to me and

saying 'Ciao Signora'. I too am a little tired of saying 'Ciao. Buongiorno!' But we all have our crosses to bear. I must say, I'd be content to be a Mystery drinker, who goes

about the place evaluating the products on offer. That could be my excuse.

But instead, work beckons and so it is that I wend my way to the school.

As I cross the six-laned road, narrowly avoiding the normal occurrence of nearly being

mowed down, I see my ancient admirer on the other side of the road, preparing to cross.

I wonder about his own safety at this point as he's not concentrating on stopping the

traffic. Instead, he shouts, 'Eh, signora! Come stai bellissima?'

Normally, I'd be flattered but with near death experiences at the forefront of my mind,

I'm more concerned with that.

'Sto bene' I respond politely, 'E lei?'

'Io sto bene aparte la gamba.' He responds.

And so it was that a conversation about the various ailments of Ernesto was relayed

across a six-laned road, amidst the perfumed fumes of traffic and the everyday shouts of

drivers.

It can take a while in Italy to realise that a fight is not about to ensue, but merely a bit of

angry banter to and fro.

And so it also was that I enquired across the road what was wrong with his leg and had he

seen a doctor.

Of all my life experiences this was definitely the first time I had ever shouted about

medical matters across a busy road.

Ernesto was, however, about to be upstaged by an elderly lady who saw no sense in

suffering fools gladly. She was for the jugular and uprighted Ernesto good and proper –

no doubt being an acquaintance of his – about his behaviour and the fact that he appeared to be deviating from that Italian thing of 'Bella Figura'.

The great thing about Ernesto is that he doesn't give a monkeys about any of that. He just does his own thing and for that reason, I feel I should call him an honorary Brit.

By the time I'd reached the tiny island in centre of the road, so had Ernesto, and so it was hard to avoid the petting of my hair without meeting my maker. As he whispered sugared words in my ear, I almost had my chance to cross, but Ernesto thought otherwise and held my arm tightly.

And so it also was that an old man enjoyed pursuing a younger woman in the midst of the craziness that is Italian traffic – and all before lunchtime.

The nuttiness of this situation for some reason reminded me of the days when my class were part of a '60s experiment. Early Sex Education delivered squarely every week on the giant school TV.

We were pretty young – a mere eight year I think – as we listened to the RP delivery of how the human species came about, with a great deal of giggling amusement.

Of course it was delivered to us in the form of diagrams with the odd explanation, but true to the times, did not even hint at the idea of extra marital relations. It was all Janet and John grown up and married.

I recall the words, 'Sometimes a man likes a woman more than just friends'. This was a new concept for us, but not one that particularly grabbed us at the time. We were more interested in the latest Beano edition.

And all of this happened before breaktime.

JANUARY 12th

When I heard that Richard Gere was in town, it seemed incongruous to say the least. I wondered what he would make of the uneven pavements and the six-laned roads; not to mention the old ladies telling him what to do. He was there to do an advert and staying in the best hotel in town. Apparently there incognito, but the Leccese cottoned on quick to this and the man was thronged from pillar to post, from Duomo to church.

It got me thinking about the relationship between Lecce and the famous, as it seems to have one.

Take for example, one marvellous celebrity who lives there and gets up to his antics. This keeps the local paper busy and nicely contrasts the latest little bomb or robbery. Of course, we didn't see him, not being prone to sheep-like behaviour, but it gave the town a bit of an oomph and the students certainly enjoyed discussing events.

It got me thinking about my autograph hunting days.

This was an early life experience and one that brought me early wisdom about how to approach and how not.

Ernesto needs lessons.

Take the time I saw a large orchestra with my father complete with famous pianist.

Of course, I wanted the autographs and so I duly waited near the dressing room at the end of their performance.

There was just one little problem. I somewhat misjudged the timing, and so it was that a ten year old girl prematurely entered the dressing room of a large group of musicians still in their underwear, changing out of their clothes!

A lesson learnt, but nonetheless autographs were procured.

It's a good job I'm not searching Lecce for autographs,. Imagine all those roads to negotiate for the six-laned beast is only one of many! I imagine the Italian autograph hunter risking life and limb as he strives for Zucchero or La Cardinale.

It must make it all the sweeter in the end.

JANUARY 14TH

How can it be that the Stracchino cheese never becomes tiresome?

In a world where too much Cheddar can tire very quickly, and the Cheesestring is utterly obnoxious, somehow Stracchino rides above it all and remains intoxicating. It does have one rival though, in my humble opinion. Gorgonzola. This cheese when found in Italy is generally soft and squidgy in consistency and not that hard stuff you sometimes find in British supermarkets. It therefore spreads pleasingly onto a nice wodge of bread and fattens you up a few calories more. The blue veins look up at you and say 'Eat me soon' and you can only comply.

A world without cheese is a sad world, in my opinion. Like some Wallace and Gromit character, I eat it with gusto. If I ever lose interest, I won't be well.

And so it was that I set off in pursuit of it, as sadly there was none to be found in the normal

Supermarket and in my rush for this delicacy, passed all the posh shops and the column procured by Sant Oronzo, from Brindisi, not to mention the numerous street vendors and dodgy road situations. That is how much I love this cheese. I would perhaps even consider travelling to the ends of the earth for it, but only if I knew they'd

saved a packet for me. One packet of the squelchy, squidgy stuff that spreads like a breeze on whatever you please.

I searched high and low, and then I found it, mooching around near some olives and at winking distance from the jar of oily artichokes, my eyes salivating already. When it finally met with the hunk of bread, I was in food nirvana and my taste buds have never been more tickled and just a few Euros.

How I miss the Lira, when to buy something you needed thousands of them. A simple panino might cost you 10,000 of the things.. It really amused me. I wonder how much it cost to buy a house !

This brings to mind the days before Decimilisation in Britain.

As a young child I was just learning about pounds, shillings and pence and the strange system in force in those days of the d. Then came the p and it all changed; confusing to say the least, but never more than for my generation.

In fact the new system was far easier but I had a resistance to it, having just mastered the old.

Isn't it always the way!

I loved the days of passport stamping too. You could show off to your friends how many exotic destinations you'd visited - the modern passport a killjoy in that respect.

Ah well.

JANUARY 15th

Oh what a beautiful morning. Impossibly I even felt a warmth on my skin as I walked down the street towards the school. I can see how this can only be an improving situation, come February and March.

The crazy guy's been lifting bins again.. He has a liking for the big ones and usually has a quick search inside before lifting the things like some weight lifter extraordinaire. With beads of sweat running down puffy red cheeks, his red jumper has stains of a substance I'd rather not ruminate on. He's an unfortunate sight next to the palms and the perfect architecture and the beautiful people who wander by or whizz on their Vespas. I notice how he is phased out by the local population. Noone seems to notice apart from me and I really notice now he's in my path and I'm not sure whether to smile or walk on by.

The baby warmth smiles on the scene and turns it comedy. Even he seems amused by his own absurdity as he lifts another bin. As if the day was to become a play, another local character appears – the one who I was told is 'alright really' but apparently shot a bunch of people some years ago and had a lengthy prison sentence. Harb. He too looks not of this time or place.

And then appears my geriatric admirer, Ernesto, who tries to woo me, in spite of being told I'm happily married, and always tries to buy my Cappuccios. He's a lonely old man, who I try to humour, but only so far as the bar exit. When he follows me down the street, the charm diminishes!

I've decided after all the madness, and indeed gentility, of Lecce, I'm going to pop away for a couple of days and see a different coloured wallpaper so I'm heading up to Barletta for a change of scene.

A quick whizz back to the flat, a gathering of clothes and freshly laundered coat, I pack my bag and charge my phone then make for the station to catch the next train up. A large lady decides to sit next to me on the train, in spite of the fact there are plenty of empty seats. This is somewhat annoying as I feel wedged in for the entire journey. I had hoped she might get off before me but she's heading to Turin, all the way. The lemony flowers and tobacco plants whizz by. Olive groves draw me in to another age, whilst the large lady peers through thick spectacles at her magazine.

Nearby, a businessman who has everything neat and pernickity down to his polished and pointy shoes, is chatting to someone he loves. His voice is loud and even though his beloved can't see, he gesticulates wildly with each morsel that pours from his mouth.

A spoilt bambino demands of his mother constantly and she ensures the little prince is adequately swathed for every whim.

Arriving at Barletta station, a slightly grim mood overtakes. The station is a home for the dispossessed and needy; the troubled and lost. That familiar juxtaposition of glamour and seedy is here too, though it is a fleeting one, as you emerge like a butterfly up the station steps to the town. It's 7 pm and already dark but I'm on the way to my hotel for the night without a care in the world.

Arriving in the foyer to a warm familiar reception, they know and welcome me as if some celebrity back home.

'Benvenuta Signora!'

I'm too tired for much attention but happy to be here so retire to bed and sleep like a baby.

JANUARY 16th

Wandering past Eraclio who stands as tall and proud as ever on Via Vittorio Emmanuelle, I

enjoy the hush of early morning as sleepy bars begin to open and wafts of coffee start to fill the air. Friends greet each other across the street or from cars, but a gentle ambience belies the crazy air that is Barletta by night.

I meander down past a couple of sleeping cats and a few lost souls to a bar not far from the

Cathedral.

A fresh new day dawning, the skies are lightly brushed with sunshine reflecting on the ancient stones of the town. Only a few tiny cotton ball clouds sprinkle the heavens whilst a yappy dog stares at me nonchalantly inside a shop that doesn't look like a shop but really is. Inside are old weighing scales and racks of vegetables and fruit which dangle appealingly from their hold. The shivering dog and its owners stare at me openly, without the English reserve I'm used to. Uncomfortable . Neither friendly nor unfriendly, they process my order for two bananas and an apple.

Across the street, the supermercato is open for business and inside I find the shouty family that run it. They're in dispute over something but have the good sense to appear calm as I enter. The old man behind the cheese counter watches me closely as I scrutinize his cheese display and drool over the sights that befall me. I also observe plump olives in small containers preserved in olive oil. He seems bemused by my fascinations and bewildered by my enthusiasms. Of course he does, for it is his whole life long and with familiarity comes ennui and ambivalence.

I am just out of the door when a crazy man walks by muttering to himself and picking up cigarette butts from the floor. He's well-dressed in typical Italian style, but not the full shilling. I am unnerved by his propensity to approach people at an alarming speed and try my best to invisible myself. As anyone who knows me will tell you, this never works for me. I'm always the one that the unsound of mind like to interact with.

Politely I sidestep his insistent attentions before making for a bar to consume my morning spremuta. It tastes a little bitter but sweet enough. A memory comes to me from corners of my mind - those 1970s fish tanks with a large paddle, that passed as Orange juice. I remember consuming said monstrosity at children's parties and school events, ever wondrous at how the liquor could taste so different from an orange. Then dawdling with the stuff at parties, even then I understood all was not as it should be.

I'm meeting my two Barlettan friends Anna and Sabina shortly for a stroll around town. They appear with huge smiles adorning their lovely faces before linking arms with me and leading me the streets.

A classic memory comes to me, near Piazza dei Caduti , of the underwear shop beneath my old flat; the one that got robbed by a gang wearing stockings on their heads! And near here another supermarket (I know them all) that was and is no more. It's the one I should either thank or blame for my Stracchino fixation for it was here some 25 years ago that I first experienced the taste of the S. It reminded me of those small packets of Walls ice-cream you used to get from sweetie shops, that were kept in exciting fridges. You'd open the wrapping all parcel and pop between wafers or into a cone. Stracchino has these exciting possibilities though spread on an Altamura panino perfection is reached. I digress.

Anna has recently had a baby and we talk awhile about the pleasures and points of motherhood as we pass the bars and cafes of the town. I have to always remember to keep my wits about me as the cars whizz by, even in the mornings, when the town is yet sleepy.

The hours pass favourably and the crazy guy has repaired to his gardens near the castle. He can be spotted at one end of the grounds sitting and rocking, as town life goes on. A Beatles song comes to mind. Who takes care of these people?

Returning to my hotel, I'm happy to see the day's newspapers displayed on poles so I sit awhile to read. It's a reminder of what a strange and deceptive place Italy can be. So glamorous on the surface, but underneath lie a multitude of sins. This darker side lurks ever ready but nonetheless suppressed by an overwhelming beauty of place and person. It's time for my siesta. I sleep and sleep and sleep. It is as if the months and years of struggle and joy and sorrow have caught up with me. When I wake it is already evening, so I read a little before returning to bed. Of course I can't sleep, so I write and think and plan and only when the dawn's pink light peers through the blinds, do I fall fast asleep again.

Tomorrow i'll return to Lecce.

JANUARY 17th

I popped into Davide's today to do photocopying and find a magazine for my bambini. There are few toys in here; small dolls and cars, but mostly just the reading material and guns. Guns for hunting. Real guns. It reminds me of an old toyshop in Lancaster that is no more, apart the weaponry wasn't real there. A rocking horse was perched above the shop and windows full of toys would draw in the eye. Stairs were rickety and uneven, but each floor would magically transport you to ever greater things, so that by the time you reached the third, you'd find the giant doll's house and the shiny bikes. I remember looking at the dolls, as a child, all boxed up for their new owner. Tiny Tears was my heart's desire. How I wanted one! It was the best because it was a drinking, weeing thing. I also had a slight predilection for the walking talking kind, but there was something eerie about the voice. You'd pull a string from its back and off it went all Zombie like across a room.

And then the games – Cluedo, Scrabble, Ludo too. Loved them all.

Ah, my magic set! Inside the box you'd find a little wand; some cards; an egg to 'disappear' and some other paraphernalia for your tricks. I'd do little shows for anyone who'd watch.

And then 'Confuscious he say'; a game bought from a Jumble Sale and Etch-a-Sketch and all. My favourite, however, was Spirograph.

How I loved the small pinned cogs and little pen patterns formed. How I loved the satisfying thrill of putting them in different ways and then creating new patterns and its inferior cousin, Spiromatic wasn't bad either, where small budding Jackson Pollocks were formed.. And not to be overlooked, my Walkie Talkie phone set. How fascinating to talk to someone in another room; though I recall quite faintly. All these toys and more made the 1960s a happy time - that and the precious time spent with my friend. Inseparable, we'd play long hours at dress up or simply watch TV. Our favourite game was Mixtures where we'd concoct recipes from the contents of mother's cupboard and then tease each other to try them. In went mustard, sugar, cocoa too and even a dab of vinegar. I still recall the awful taste, but to we children it was such fun. How happy we were to pootle about or paddle around at the beach. We even went to Drama lessons and performed in plays where we'd giggle backstage and even on. Some seven years this was to last, until stuff pulled the friendship apart.

Time and all that jazz. Different schools.

And so, as I look at the toys in Davide's shop, I feel that sense of wonderment again, of childhood lost and innocence and the sight of toy shop treasures.

JANUARY 18th

Strange songs from the '60s keep wafting through my head today 'Ta ra la bumpteeay' or 'Let's drink a drink a drink to Lily the Pink'. What on earth were they about? As a child it was all frankly puzzling. It's so strange to review your life and think how it has changed since childhood. How long ago since we were told not to play any more with Clackers in the playground. Nay, parents were not to buy them anymore. Children were singing 'Yellow

submarine' at playtime and my friend Alison and I would jump around on her Hopper after school and watch the tortoise.

I think we were hoping it might do something spectacular but, comforted by the ensuing routine, it never did. We enjoyed pottering around to get it choice Dandelion leaves and it

seemed to display a certain enthusiasm for these. Alison's mother made her a pink wet-look mac and I wanted one too. My mother bought me a navy one, which seemed perfunctory but was acceptably wet in its appearance. Alison was my best friend ever though and a very good introduction to the bonds of friendship, for she was sweet, funny and loyal.

We would send each other postcards from our summer holidays and I remember being fascinated by the one from Switzerland with its glaciers. It was maybe this very postcard that alerted me to the fact that there were more exciting places in the world than Lancashire. However, the Spanish ones really enthralled with their warm golden sands and colourful beach furniture. I couldn't imagine anything nicer than to be there in the warmth by a shimmering sea.

These early memories were a slowly forming movement that became my interest in travel abroad and all that goes with it. It wasn't until Italian classes in 1985, however, that this became more of a reality. Actually, I should rewind to 1984 when i spent two weeks on the sunny island of Corfu. So taken I was with the quality of the light, the aroma of herbs, flowers and limpid sea, that I don't think I was ever quite the same again. In fact, at one time, the furthest I'd truly wished for was the town of my birth, good old Londinium.

How times had changed.

Corfu, then Italian lessons led me to a chance encounter that would completely alter the course of my life. Grizzly Graziella the teacher had to return to Italy only to be replaced by Francesco, who took us on a class visit to Bologna. We made good our escape to the seaside town of Comacchio where every word uttered brought me to my senses.
Romance.

A year and a half later I was married and living in Bologna. Even this seems a lifetime ago as I ponder on the course my life has taken to date.

So now I sit on my return train to Lecce in a mostly empty carriage. A young couple sit together with their toddler, an air of boredom emanating, past the olive groves and the lemony flowers, the clear blue seas of the Adriatic. An elderly couple get on at Bari and smile with old-fashioned gentility.

I miss the days when Italy was more like this.

The warmth and affability used to grab you tangibly but these days the majority are as anywhere – aloof and indifferent. Perhaps it's just my age but I think it's more to do with the age – that of mass media and homogenisation.

Everywhere is anywhere is nowhere.

Arriving in Lecce, the first thing I notice is how classy the station seems after Barletta. Very classy indeed. The second is how the buildings stand majestic in their Baroque sandy tones and how the warmth of the January sun is already gracing all it touches.

In my nostalgias I'm struck how on arriving back at my flat, my whole life has led me to this point. For I am here in my kitchen with a small pan of water and a lighter bought from a street vendor, waiting for the water to boil, preparing a cup of tea and applying slivers of cheese to my panino. I am here. This is where I am and this is how it is.

JANUARY 19th

Happy, happy, happy, happy... That song keeps whirring round my head on a loop. Earworm. It doesn't seem to go with the newspaper headlines, but I suppose even a few mug shotted folk might have had their moments.

I do wonder about the bird-like old lady I see wondering around. She doesn't have Dementia, but she says some strange things. I don't think she's happy but I bet she once was.

So it's still early in the year, but somehow I don't feel quite in the winter zone, even though it is cool. Viale Japigia isn't happy. It has a kind of tired look about it, but up there, on a shop terrace I can see a palm tree and it's a fully functioning one.

Regardless the tree, I have to photocopy some farm animals for the kiddies. Davide's is quiet and so I'm able to do it with ease. This is unusual, not because the place is always full, but because I'm used to obstacles. I've had this thing for a while where I need to go

from A to B via Z to get to C.

Take the opening a bank account thing.

Sounds straightforward enough, but you need this, that and the other until you give up.

As for bank transfers, forget it. Just starve. It's easier. They did tell me something about

a place on a back street near Piazza Sant'Oronzo, but when I entered the joint, it felt

about as sensible as a teenager to proceed, so I didn't.

I wonder if it will ever get sorted, you know, this life thing. The practicalities.

The bird-like lady meanders about the school bar nervously. I'd love to know her story.

It must be fascinating.

So, as I start my lessons, I hear a strange noise outside. I know not what it is and it is not

of this world, or so it seems to me. The whirring, spindly sound, all rattle snake, is

bugging me as I try to convey the delicate matter of the Simple Past. The Simple Past is

not simple if you are not a native speaker. It is very simple if you are. There are a lot of

'I have bought some bread at ten oclocks' to contend with. Agh! How I try to clarify,

but the whirring and spindling and rattly noise is driving me insane. On asking the

students, they merely shrug their shoulders in gallic fashion. I can tell you that at 11.30

pm that evening I was still lying in my bed trying to work it out. To this day I know not

what it was. It reminds me of my snake on the beach experience in '89. I still have no

valid explanation. It's a strange facet of Italy that some things are a complete mystery

and you will never, ever know.

JANUARY 20th

The man's sitting in a black car on my road again. It makes me uneasy. This isn't simply a driver resting awhile. I can't quite make him out but he sits and stares across the street to a palazzo entrance, engine off. He sits, waits and cuts a sinister figure.

I've met another. Similar. In a shop.

I've seen it often. And so as I wander towards Dok, I pretend not to notice, then round the corner bump right into Signora Rizzi. Which is more troubling is hard to say!

'Buongiorno Signora,' She says all Queen Bee.

'Buongiorno!' I reply.

'Mi raccomando. You should use the lift.'

It is pointless to try and explain, so I don't; smile weakly and carry on.

She's a woman on a mission, you see. A handbag warrior.

When I reach Dok, the young beggar's sitting in the doorway with a cup. With bloated features, he looks perhaps twenty and quite unwell. Always polite, I pop a Euro into his cup or two. I once bought him something to eat, but he looked at it as if it were poison and so won't be trying that again.

JANUARY 21st

Another day. A crispy dawn wakens me from my slumber as light seeps through the slats of my blinds. I can hear a jangling sound from some unidentified object, swaying in the wind. I can hear voices outside, but it's only the voices of the early birds on their start. Today will be quite long as I have many lessons.

A smile warms my face as I slip into the shower and prepare for my day. Sleepy but excited, I munch on a packeted Cornetto from Dok.

Tripping to school, I bump into one of my fellow teachers. We're not naturally attuned, partly due to the age gap, so happily proceed on our way and then I spot Ernesto, my ancient admirer. I decide to pop into the Perfumery at this point to escape his attentions but this is to prove costly. Here I waste five minutes trying this scent or that until I find just the one. 'Onde Mystere'. The shop assistant insists it's for me and I agree wholeheartedly spraying all pulse points with natural enthusiasm. Some forty-five Euros worse off, I'd forgotten about Ernesto, so caught up in my senses at the gorgeous fragrance. Then I bump right into him. Of course, his radar had scented me and he'd waited patiently outside.

'Ma Signora, you smell divine!'

'Thank you,' I blush before trying to jemmy my way down a side street towards the school.

'You've been buying the perfume' he says, as if I'd done so for him.

'It suits you. Andiamo per un bel caffè'

Awkwardly, I walk towards the school when I can make my excuses and hotfoot it to class. I felt great though. The heady scent had brought summer a little closer and I breezed through the day, smelling literally of roses.

And then a little exhaustion after lesson five or so. A droop of spirits. A quick Espresso and my crazy class. Anna is on top form. She's singing today and then accompanies with small dance routine on the desk - in her 40s and bags of fun.

How we laugh!

By 9 I am wiped out. My perfume a distant memory and all the summer buzz a pleasant yesterday. Heading back across the six-laned traffic fumes, I want another spray of the delicious elixir, if only to recapture the finer things.

I quickly concoct one 'Penne all Pomodoro' sprinkled with nubs of Gorgonzola and drizzled with Olive oil.

Deliciousness.

A little bread dabbed in the tomato juices exquisite. A drink of milk. Bath. Read.

Sleep. ZZzz.

JANUARY 22nd

I leave the flat early for the shops. Passing the mustard building to my left, along the small side street near my flat, there's something about the colour that reminds me of my past. 1979 in London. Working as Temp at the Royal Free in Hampstead, I remember the hurried departure and my mother's pained expression. I was young , just 18,and had never been away from home before, yet here I was suddenly declaring my intention to move the very next day. Impulsively. And so I stood on some motorway sidewalk with my boyfriend hitching a lift to the big city. Seemed exciting at the time. The jobs came easily too; the travelling not. I recall the multiple transport experience and the descent into the bowels of the tube, and all this before 8.30 of the morning. I also remember returning to London from a Christmas break to find we'd been moved out, near Alexandra Palace. Pre mobile phones, with no way of contacting my boyfriend, I wandered lonely and scared on pavements and towards a friend's place and sat crying on the upper deck of a Muswell Hill bus. Then, to my astonishment, my boyfriend got on the same bus, so all was well in the end. Amazing. Big city London. We slept on a library floor then moved to Camden where I got the job.

So why the mustard yellow link?

Because we lived awhile in a large hotel with mustard yellow windows. It was a crazy place with strangest of characters inside. Within its walls, the one who popped up from the cellar with daily wisdoms, and the one who popped down from the attic; the mysterious South African and the couple in identical clothing. All eccentric and strange. I recall the multiple munching of toast and the cupfuls of cheery coffee before work and the small Tandoori restaurant nearby. A launderette for coins sat listlessly beside and behind the hotel, some wasteland, like a magical garden gone wrong.

I remember the phone calls home and the evenings out. London '79. And I was 18, just. And so I pass the mustard house and don't think fondly of the days I'd enter Finefare and hear 'Gonna get along without you now' or 'Spooky little girl' on the radio. I just feel sad for my mother. She must have worried.

I was strong as an ox back then, lugging a case as big as me to the tube and on to Euston. Saw John Le Mesurier in the crowd. He looked just as in role. And then the long journey home, back from the chaos of the capital.

I'm lost in memories at this point, but then spot Ernesto, my ancient admirer, in hot pursuit:

'Quanto sei bella!' He tells me, with a twinkle in his eye.

'Dove vai?' I tell him that I'm off to Dok and he walks beside uninvited. He knows everyone as we pass and looks as pleased as punch.

When we reach the strange piazza near the supermarket, I manage to take my leave by entering a dress shop and here I pause awhile to look at the expensive creations that someone else will buy and then I brave the outside once again, past the begging lady and the chatty teens. Schlooped inside the supermarket, I buy plump vine tomatoes, some Pecorino; a packet of Farfalle and some fancy fish. It comes to a pretty penny then, with stuff precariously balanced in inadequate bags, I head for my flat.

As I walk, along, I assume that Ernesto's long gone, but I'm wrong...

I see him sitting in the square. Waiting. And so I walk on, hoping he won't notice and as luck has it, get sandwiched in a tourist group, all gaggle of geese, and carried along towards the President Hotel. He's still looking in the direction of Dok, and I'm on my way. I wave to the bank guard then make my way into the flat.

Around 3.40, I head to the school, dodging traffic as normal. I overhear some snippet of conversation about animal entrails left on some shop doorstep. It sounds sinister, and is. I walk on. The uneven stones beneath my feet insecure, then round past the bar where they're always tipsy and on and on and on to the corner cafe. In the throne with my paper, I survey the world from the comfortable chair.

The scent of my Espresso wafts vaguely up, as I read the latest atrocities in 'Il Quotidiano', then my eyes catch sight of two impeccable leather brogues and a walking stick.

'Ma Signora, how did you get back from Dok?'

Ernesto the ancient admirer stands before me, and he's not about to relent. Luckily, it's time for work and so I pass him a gallic shrug and make my way into the sanctuary of school.

JANUARY 23rd

Siesta time. Relaxed, I lie and ponder life's intricacies when suddenly, as if a giant has taken hold of the entire bed, a violent shake whilst the ceiling lamp swings recklessly from side to side. Disorientated in the early moments I think of vibrating washing machines and other logical explanations. I even wonder if I'm fitting. But then, of course, I realise it's the tremors of an earthquake rattling me to the core. Unused to such occurrences, I remark to the newsagent later who looks nonplussed. Here they are commonplace, the epicentre often Greece. I feel it quite severely as I'm on the fifth floor and find that others haven't felt it at all. When will it strike again? I feel uneasy. Re-living it in my memory: The closing of my eyes and gentle sound of music from somewhere, then suddenly, as if two giant hands had taken my bed and angrily tossed it about. Such a peculiar sensation. The rattling and clinking of the crockery and glass; the rumblings and tremblings and unsteadiness.

At first the dogs are quiet. Too quiet. But then they bark. I recall that one barked just before. Perhaps it knew.

And so from this day on, my feet feel less part of me and even less attached to the ground. My physical being, a light careless thing that's not mine to control. As I walk around, I start to wonder. When?

I soon realise the locals are far more concerned with rain – and with good reason. Often torrential, it causes huge problems: People have drowned in underground car parks even. The infrastructure is not always compatible with health and safety here.

JANUARY 24th

We've moved well away from Christmas now and those dark days before. The quality of light is ever brighter and the sun seems to warm a little more each day. At night I still clasp my hot water bottle to me like an old woman, although they all seem to burst on me. The first time was shocking, What an indignity it was! Since then I have regarded the rubber bottle with due caution. I don t trust them any more having had a coddled childhood where the bottle never seemed to burst.

When I enter the school, it seems too warm as the heating is on and direct heat is not something my flat is acquainted with. My flat is not acquainted with anything but an arguing couple; a rotation of tenants and a tidy landlord who loves to potter.

My students are great and I always like to remember that. No matter how crazy the wandering lost or how cold the flat, my students are warm, kind and funny.

Seeing them this morning has reminded me of my favourite new eaterie. A delicatessen that sells seafood pasta with tiny octopus and clams intermingled with a lemon parsley sauce that swaddles each strand.   I will scoff it for my lunch. But who do I espy in the shop as I walk towards it? Two people of my knowledge. One, a fellow student who grins amiably at me as we share this naughty habit. Two, it s the 'He's alright really but...' aka HARB who now wanders the streets with an away look in his eyes.

The latter puts me off the idea completely and I plump instead for a pizza slice in the local supermercato. I could cook today but I've so much to do and so little time. Not only that but the lighter doesn't work any more and try as I might I can't spot any street vendors today. I usually see them everywhere wodged full of them.

In my flat, I notice that the kitchen has been changed with the chairs neatly placed under the table.

A nasty looking envelope sits on the table and one big fat One Electricity bill that reminds me of home... I try not to panic at the thought and carry on with my pizza slice whilst feeling vaguely stupid for avoiding my delicatessen over a multiple murderer. Lessons need to be planned and I set to with a will. It's that time again and I scurry to the school, bag in hand and shades poised for the brightening sun. The bank guard looks depressed today. Maybe he just got his Electricity bill too or maybe he too had to forego the joys of the deli. On second thoughts, I don't think the multiple murderer would phase him at all.

I walk on, past the shops, including the one where they were delivered of an unpleasant package recently, until I spot Ernesto, my ancient admirer, walking as fast as he can in my direction with his walking stick. I try to gesture that I am in speed, but he has deaf ears and follows me like a lamb to the bar. 'Quanto sei bella!' He croons as I try to remember my lesson plan and avoid slurping my Cappuccio too fast. The lovely laundry ladies come in, as they always do, and have probably done so for centuries. Their routines are comforting in this strange world where you can never fully relax. With heightened senses, I purvey the view to see how many mad people or animals are about. Thankfully only me.

Carpe diem.

JANUARY 25th

After shopping, I hop into a taxi. The driver's female and no-nonsense. She scolds me for not alerting her the street in time so we do a loopy loop for five seconds to the right place. She's alright. A type.

They are all still outside the corner bar as ever. I imagine in amusement that they'd never left and are permanent fixtures - the one with the soft brogues; the one with the tan. They all look incredibly wealthy, but you can never really tell. Bella figura you see. And then, as if to prove a point I see the bin lifter again. It isn't difficult to explain what he's doing and he's doing it a lot. Noone bats an eye. It's just another cog in the wheel. Perhaps if he wasn't lifting bins, they'd bat that eye.

I repair to my flat, quite tired after the lugging, and lie on my bed looking up at the flecked ceiling. I'm not sure why, after two cappuccinos, but I fall fast asleep and wake up hours later. By then the street life below is buzzing and loud. A shouting man disturbs me. I didn't understand the Italian but I know it wasn't good. And so, I decide to just stay inside and acclimatize. I have a treasured Altamura panino still and some Gorgonzola cheese. Just enough milk for a tea and a bag of pasta, besides a tin of tomatoes from Dok, and all is well with the world.

I thought to sit on my balcony a while, but then I saw the family opposite doing same. This felt uncomfortable; like peering into someone's front room, so I retired to read a book.

I've never been an afternooner. Too much commotion and too many vibes. I prefer the quiet cool of morning, when the only voices are greeters on their way to work or the cats a calling

or the birds a twittering. Few people. I like it like this.

It seems a shame to waste the day, but sometimes it is good, to just rest. We are not always good at this, attaching guilt to inactivity, but for me it was a tonic. I popped again on the balcony to see what was happening, but no sooner than I saw a street gang near the corner. They didn't look pleasant, so I went back inside and returned to my book. I missed home today - the English ambience and green fields. I missed my loved ones and my streets. I missed the sense of belonging and the sense of home. I wondered if I'd made a

mistake in coming here. Sometimes isolation's the word. An empty aching loneliness pervades. 'I need a crowd of people, but I can't face them day to day', an old Neil Young song.

Very old. The walls seemed to agree.

But food has a way of rectifying these sad moods. And so it was that a bowl of chilli tomato

dabbed with bread became my saviour for the day - that and a phone call home. Although I dislike phone calls generally, there are times when you have to reconnect. So I did.

It wasn't such a bad feeling. The aftermath of all. I knew the next day would be different. Each day is the new year, I tell myself, with fresh hopes and plans. Always.

JANUARY 26th

An extraordinary day lies ahead for me today. One of my students – a film maker has invited to a casting day, not as potential actress, I must add, but simply to watch and enjoy the proceedings and so I'm more glamorous than usual for I'm to be whisked off to the casting.

As my escorts lead me though Lecce by car to the casting venue, I feel like a celebrity racing to the Oscars. Daft really. So here I would sit with a film crew. A cameraman would film each actor in turn whilst the director and his colleagues would make their decisions. All this was to happen before 4pm and my tiny tots English lesson.

As each hopeful appeared with the aim to impress, I realised that empathy can go too far. No you can't take them all on, I reasoned to myself, yet they all seemed so talented. To my embarrassment, some would focus on impressing me, yet I had no say and so it should be. I tried to show support in my eyes then wondered if this would mislead and give false hope. A fascinating experience nonetheless till dutifully whisked back to the corner bar, opposite my school for cappuccino. I felt like Cinderella back home again, but a new dimension had been added to my world; one with interesting moments and strange twists and turns.

Watching the four year olds in my class was like observing a different film altogether. This lot are to be cast in that greatest film of all - the future. Life with all its moments and surprises; its sads and happys. Right now they are oblivious to all that will come but I see they will fit aptly into their role – that of destiny. Che sera sera. A destiny of bella figura, good coffee and great style, with a few bumps here and there no doubt, but nothing to write home about. They are Italy's children at the fortunate end of things, as all are from good homes and loving families. Si vede. Lucky them!

JANUARY 28th

First thing, I pop into the Deutschebank to get some Euros for my remaining Sterling; the ones I brought back from England at Christmas. The man looks at my cash as if it has a disease, and it's not for the changing. I rush into school in a flurry and flounce through my lessons. Today it's the Imperfect and it is imperfect, every bit of it. Noone gets it. That's my responsibility and I must find a way to present it better. After class I rush to another bank with my precious notes. They too look with disdain at them and I begin to wonder if they think it's Monopoly money. Ach it's nearly February and I still haven't managed to change the blasted things. I think I'll just keep them till Easter homing.

I definitely want a trip into town today for I have things to do and I want to acquaint myself with the local banks. It's here that I see a plethora of street vendors all equipped with at least ten lighters. I am so happy to see them, but then an awful truth dawns. I have no cash on me! I left it at the flat. With the vague idea to hotfoot it back it seems a little daft, so I simply, with a resigned air, have a Cappuccio with the few coins I do have on me, and sit back .

I have now been here nearly four months and I'm none the wiser. On the surface all is serene and calm. All is certainly aesthetically pleasing and the little yappy dogs seem to attest to a certain laissez faire in the air.

The posh and the humble shops alike all have their place and their dignity stands unparalleled. Noone lacks self-esteem in this place. Confidence seems to ooze from each and every pore.

Even the pets would agree.

I am the only 'outsider' in sight and certainly the only one buying postcards from the tourist office by the Duomo. I look at the Baroque images and wonder how the pictures were caught as mine never look so good. With minimal time before closing, I hurry back to the flat. When I arrive I realise I need some milk so pop out to the local shop with my cash, only to see a street vendor with lighter. I'm overjoyed and buy one and feel blessed as I throw together olive oil, garlic and tomatoes to concoct a simple yet perfect dish. It

hits the spot, along with a wodge of Stracchino.   I hope that wasn't a scorpion I just saw

scuttling up the wall behind the cooker, I'd rather not know. Far too busy to worry about

such things.

Let the scorp be and maybe it'll do the same.

I feel happy. No idea why. Spring must be in the air.

CHAPTER FIVE - FEBRUARY

FEBRUARY 2nd

There's a nip in the air as I head along Via Oberdan with its many shops and apartments

lined up all chocolate box. The vegetable one has Altamura Panini freshly in so I buy the

warm, scented bread which is placed briskly into a crisp paper bag. On my return, whilst

I wait for a typical day to unfold, the landlord enters with urgent tones. I am to move

from this flat as he's selling up before the week is out. In that way which sudden

unwanted news strikes us, I reel and look aghast around my room at the myriad things

strewn about

 – books, files, clothes have formed alliances with toothpaste and Aqua e Sapone bags.

How will I move all this stuff between lessons and , more to the point, where shall I move

it to? As I flitter about trying to rack up solutions, the landlord re-enters.

He'd forgotten to add something.

I could move to his other flat round the corner so it's not to be a problem and, stranger

still, from the kitchen window, I can even see it. I will love my sunny balcony, he says,

and my flat-mates. It 's all so easy.

Too easy.

I stand at the window in mute fascination at the vision that will become my new home; a place I must have looked at many times without 'seeing' it. It isn't far but enough to make discerning details tricky so I can just see a curtain flapping in the breeze by two brown shuttered doors, a small table with perhaps an ashtray, and an empty plant pot. I begin to imagine my version of this space and it isn't an unpleasant thought. It 's on the fourth floor I see, and faces another apartment block near concreted ground where once was a building that is no more.

Beside this an underground car park and further still the main road, Viale Japigia, where I risk life and limb on a daily basis to reach my school. As the day wears on, I even begin to warm to the idea and as I sip my pre-school Cappuccino, daydream how my new room will be and how I will no longer need to listen to my shouty neighbours. Every cloud ..

FEBRUARY 3rd

The February light's intoxicating. Gilded, it dances with potted plants on sunny balconies. There's no wind, apart a gentle breeze here and there rustling my yellowed curtains.

Maria and Mariella are meeting me for lunch today and I'm looking forward. A sad dog yaps in the distance - I try to ignore because it upsets me, but I can sense it's unhappy. As I wander along Via Oberdan, a mother strolls with two young children. They are a little naughty and she scolds them, but I can see she's a good and doting mother. The tiny boy babbles in fledgeling Italian whilst mamma keeps a grip on one wriggling hand. Heading into the centre, there are small dogs galore. It seems to be a fashion here. The petite pooch clings uncomfortably to its glamorous owner and seems an extension of their wardrobe. I doubt that it gets much attention behind closed doors; though perhaps I'm wrong.

Nearly 10 and the streets are filling with early starters - some in cars, others on bikes. Some even sit on pavements working Scratch cards. An ubiquitous gaggle of teenagers hang around near McDonald's; to me an eyesore, but they seem rather drawn. Piazza Sant'Oronzo is essentially strange. With its Roman amphitheatre juxtaposing modernity, as well as the column; its frequent exhibitions and happenings flecked with balloons, not forgetting its ancient tree (some 500 years I believe), it's a hotchpotch kind of a place. Perhaps, dare I add, not too attractive.

McDonald's sits stubbornly to one side, near the book shop and the postcard stalls. A small kiosk nearby sells newspapers galore. Then several large cafes deliver the goods; the sweetmeats and the coffee that form many a rushed breakfast.

There is a bank nearby and this reminds me of the saga that awaits the hapless tourist. Once entered, you may need to switch off your watch and retire. The process can be excruciating and finally when you reach the desk, they can't give you what you need. This happened to me in northern Puglia once. As I recall, we were given numbers (like an Argos queue) and that was that. We were left to rot.

I mooch around the book shop awhile, reading the blurbs of one or another and smile at the assistant to facilitate the lifting of some tome or other. It reduces their paranoia. Then, re-emerging onto the square to dazzling light, I see Maria across the way and we head to a cafe to meet Mariella.

These two women were born and bred here, so I get a potted history and the pride they both feel shows in every gesture. It goes beyond mere words, however, as they're involved in city

projects to promote and support the place; both in terms of cultural events and all matters archaeological. They tell me about the Faggiano family who found a veritable museum beneath their house, after some mundane problem down below. There it all was ...Roman vases, artefacts and even a hole used by Franciscan nuns to mummify dead bodies. How amazing that must have been!

Mariella's friend is a tour guide here so many means and ways can be found to know Lecce better.

Soon hunger takes over and we head to our eaterie, a nearby trattoria. The reserved waitress takes our orders, after some ponderance. For me Bruschetta and then the Tagliattelle ai Funghi. A slight disapproval crosses my friends' brows. Such simple peasant food to an Italian, but to me, divine. In fact I am saddened how creativity has changed menus here to strange concoctions so far removed from simple plates I recall. It is in fact the Funghi dish that I remember from bygone times. 1986 if I'm correct. Lovely it was. However, this was soon surpassed by one gooey Gorgonzola, that coated each strand to perfection. My traditional fare may not impress my friends, but it impresses me. Delicious. Bruschetta. The plump scarlet tomatoes meld with olive oil and go down nicely on toasted bread, with just a hint of aglio. By the time dessert comes, I fall back on tradition. Tiramisu can't be beaten, nor should it. The coffee-infused Amaretto hits the spot so we stay awhile chatting about family stuff; our hopes and even our dreams. I confide of my move and all the machinations therein. The disappointments are to follow the post prandial Espressos. And then we walk along sundrenched streets, admiring the Baroque of this building or that. It's only 2 by the time we part, but I have a busy evening's lessons ahead. Strolling back to my flat, a tourist moment takes me so I buy a postcard. Nothing special, but something to send home. It features the Duomo and catches my eye; all yellows, beiges and blues and then I bump into a student and we chat awhile about stuff and nonsense before I finally make it 'home'.

Then I remember.

I need photocopies and there's little time. The lazy dawdle into sprint sees books and pages scrabbled feverishly to the appropriate place. Davide obliges. Thank goodness he exists.

FEBRUARY 4th

It's a sad thing here to find the town so full of young African street vendors. I feel and fear for them. Some look too young to be dealing with the stresses and strains of modern street life, but I guess they have little choice. Sometimes they seem happy but mostly just alone and vulnerable. At other times, these young men can be aggressive, desperate to sell you something, but I realise this is their anxiety; and their survival. Sometimes it really saddens me how they must have suffered and I wonder what they've left behind. Do they cry themselves to sleep at night? I think not. I know because a pain so deep often gets suppressed.

This, in sharp contrast to the happy faces around me gracing the Leccese streets. Here youngsters are generally well fed and clothed; a sense of affluence and wealth, even privilege. And so, as I wander the streets, I notice the differences but also the similarities. A young African jokes with his friend, just like any Italian boy, but without the nice home to return to. I like to give to them, as gesture of solidarity and care. Like a two-tiered world, the Leccese go about their business and mostly ignore. Perhaps some care but I feel the pendulum swings mostly to indifferent.

So here I am, another fish out of water, belonging neither here nor there and not needing to belong. The sallow face of an old man looks across at me from a bar. The face belongs to an

impeccable outfit, complete with hat. The hands are an old dark brown pair and he peers through thick lenses at the world. I muse how it must have changed for him over the years and how his early life must have been. Si vede. Everything about him suggests time- honoured tradition, even down to the leather bag beside him. I wonder about his days as a young man.

Maybe he knows Ernesto, the ancient admirer. Maybe he's had a sad life and become a widower. There's a sorrow hanging over him I can't quite place. Perhaps his traditional life didn't go entirely as expected, aside the regular pasta meals of course, and then I ruminate that perhaps he was a maverick, eschewing the traditions placed before him and that maybe this lead to his alienation: much like the street vendors. But then I see a young woman approaching him and they greet, link arms and wander off down the street. There is a tangible warmth between them. Padre e figlia? I'm not sure, but I'm sure that his life has been as expected, no errant at all.

Then I see a little dog, a yappy little thing all pretty in its pink leather collar, like some lady of the night, but the small beast looks sad. What is it about Lecce that gives this air of sorrow amidst the glamour, wealth and endless Baroque beauty? A certain hollowness or emptiness is perceptible; sometimes in the eyes and sometimes in the light and even sometimes in me, yet my students ooze happiness and inner joy. This contradiction fascinates me; a light in their eyes against an emptiness in the streets.

And what of perception?

How curious it would be to see the world through another's eyes. Perhaps it would be like upping the volume or looking through a veiled curtain.

Like death, this is surely something we must struggle to know. I also wonder how it would be to know oneself as another person. This impossible quest, along with all the other impossibilities and inevitabilities seem to little avail.

Narrowly avoiding another encounter with a fast car, I reflect how close we always are to death; like stepping through a door.

All this reflection is soon swept aside as I enter my kiddie class. Little Maria decides to buzz around Mario causing a merry scene. A calm story and colouring in just about resolves it. Perhaps I'm not entirely suited to this age group and certainly prefer my adult classes.

How could I not enjoy the humorous banter of my over 40s? They are beyond hilarious, and I'm thankful for it.

FEBRUARY 5th

Tomorrow I'll be moving to my new room. A sense of apprehension grips me. Luckily the shouty couple are in fine form today making my impending escape all the sweeter. I glance from the kitchen to my new home and then groan as I turn to face the packing to be done. I will need sustenance for the task and what better than one sticky Cornetto and Cappuccino to give energy. The corner bar is full of regulars, tastefully sipping on Espressos and small sweetmeats. These glamorous, well-heeled folk chat animatedly, though some read with intense concentration the latest financial report or daily news, through expensive glasses, with fine lined jackets to snug in. I feel ready for the task ahead and jog up the five flights to my flat. This will be one of the last times I enter it; a thought which doesn't displease.

Now positively enthused at the move, I race the place, popping paraphernalia into suitcase and bag; a clean here and there as I warm to the change. After a couple of hours, all is good to go and I already have the keys to my new place. I decide to take a few items, just to christen my new home.

Managing to enter the palazzo with one of many new keys, I'm encouraged by the sweet smell of regular cleaning alongside an elegantly placed potted plant near the portone. Tiny wooden boxes, each with ancient printed names and some so faded as to suggest long term residents, are to be the new post box. An old lamp completes a charming picture of decades past. A businessman impeccably clad rushes by politely as I wander unpolished stairs.

'There's a lift!' Offers a kindly old lady as I climb up, but without the judgemental tones of La Rizzi, meno male. As for lifts, I've heard some horror stories, one such being the stricken lift traveller who had the strength of mind to go into deep zen meditation after being inside for 48 hours.. What else could you do? The ancients red alarm buttons rarely work; folk too busy to care.

Noone takes responsibiltily.

Arriving at the right door, upon entering, I see an interesting coat hanger that takes pride of place. The hallway has a marble floor with mirror on the main door which I observe to be a flattering and elongating one. To my amusement, It has a strange floral design which will feature in some humorous photos on a Triffid theme.

Then Natalie appears.

She's smoking a cigarette and, still in her dressing gown, says 'Hello' dismissively to this new arrival. This evacuee. I understand her. She can't be bothered. A mop is propped by the kitchen wall and she sets to with a vengeance and quickly tells me where everything is then swishes back to her cleaning before hogging the bathroom. I feel vaguely uneasy but turn a shiny silver key into my new room. It is strange. I am absolutely without words ...

FEBRUARY 6th

All moved in and fascinated by the Triffid mirror, I begin to sort out my room. Natalie has

apologized for the cigarette butts on my balcony; the chaise-long that doubled up as doggy bed and the dog hairs. I am unfazed nor care about such things but she knows me not. Returning from Dok with cleaning products, I cannot love my walls. Are they Asbestos I wonder? Hopefully not. They are strange and of a gritty texture. The white undulations are nothing, however, when compared to the strange space-age wardrobe which hovers precariously above the bed, and is all about Italian style. This, I learn on my first night, when I awake only to bump my head quite fiercely on the wardrobe perched above. My bed is to be banished from its nest and placed further out, though this does alter the aesthetics of the room, which will doubtless displease the landlord's wife. My attempts to avoid head injuries will be futile as it will be moved back into its perfect location discreetly next day, to my dismay.

To my left is an old-fashioned record player and across, a desk with broken lid. Above, implanted into the textured wall are two book shelves which prove useful. I hear a key turning and surmise that Natalie is around so go to peep. It isn't Natalie but the other flat-mate, who turns out to be a Danish dancer, Anna. She compliments the darkened hall with gleaming blonde hair and pale skin. Her English impeccable, she has a warm, reserved manner. I like her and feel glad she's around. Natalie emerges from the bathroom with a swoosh and heads for the kitchen. From here she leans smoking from a window, mobile in hand. I repair to my balcony and notice a cat on the one below amidst the potted plants, tables, chair, some shoes and a washing line. It snuggles into its bed and seems oblivious to the cool air. And then I'm summoned to the kitchen by Natalie. She looks angry and nervously smokes a cigarette. It seems our landlord is trying to sell this place too so we can't stay long. She also informs me that the letting agent is a frequent visitor along with potential buyers. Angry and exasperated, she explains how every day by noon she leaves to avoid all the interruptions and rarely returns till after 8 when noone will come. My first reaction sympathy, a second, worry. My third a shared exasperation. I've just moved in and my muscles still sore from the carrying and lifting but I guess it will take a while. I am only here till June, after all ...

FEBRUARY 7th

As slats of light seep through my blinds, I lay awhile in bed, enjoying the sensation of duvet against skin and stretch like a cat into the day. Soon the small pan's a bubbling for my tea and I'm looking through the kitchen window at the roof tops below and the rising sun, blessing a yellow dawn dappled with palest blue. I watch a man leave his palazzo and enter his workaday car whilst another is cleaning the street. I'm on the fourth floor so they're not aware as I watch them, in miniature, as the early day begins.

I'm fascinated by a small garden below. Amidst the endless concrete palazzi, the TV aerials and the roads, sits one perfect patch of greenery. It has a tree and a small child's swing which looks abandoned. An old tricycle lies on the grass and a palm sways gently. What a perfect image of sanctuary, like peering through a port-hole to an island. It is also somehow quintissentially English as if an English garden has been plonked in one built up southern Italian town. The garden 's alluring, yet seems untouched, as if forgotten in the everyday cogs of life. I wonder about the animal life there. Would there be snakes? Perhaps. A cat would probably sit beneath the shaded tree. Possibly a lizard or two would perch upon a rock. I imagine the garden by the sea and opening that gate to golden dunes by pristine seas. I realise that it's out of place, this garden. Like the street vendors and me, it doesn't belong.

FEBRUARY 8th

I think the old man living nearby must have passed. A lot of relatives can be heard in the flat and the tones are sombre and sad. I don't see him so I'm guessing. I step out into bright sunshine which makes me sad and reminds me of my mother's funeral; a beautiful spring day which made it so more poignant somehow, as she loved Spring. Yet soon I am greeted by the cheerful pair in the posh veg shop and all such gloom evaporates.

I need to do some shopping today so heading for Dok, past the street vendors and the peculiarities of Piazza Mazzini, I trot downstairs and, Euro placed in trolley, release it for its round. Soon filled with Tea, Milk, Fruit and Veg, I head for the most important part – the cheese counter. How I love to look at all the different types displayed there with irrefutable charm. In spite of a million varieties,

I plump for Stracchino again, plus a smidgeon of wholesome Pecorino. If I was a cheese, I'd be Stracchino and there it is. There's a palpable air of anxiety in here. Everyone rushes and check out is excruciating. Schloop! My shopping goes down a mini-chute then into its endlessly breakable bag. Up the steps, and already imagining the Stracchino experience, I bump into none other than Ernesto, my ancient admirer.

'Ma Signora, come stai?'

I try to be polite but being a little tired, find myself a little curt. Ernesto the ancient admirer

doesn't notice and proceeds .

'Let me carry your bags for you,' he croons. 'I could drive you home.'

Not on your nelly.

I manage to make my excuses and move faster than the norm in the right direction with a quick and cheery wave. Ernesto seems none the wiser but I guess he'll never learn.

Past the peculiarities of Piazza Mazzini, the posh shops; the chemist with friendly waving assistant; two or three roads and round past Davide's to my new flat, I stroll.

A sinister character is hanging near a shop.

I don't look for long and proceed through the keyed gate, along a path to the grand portone, then in again past the ancient letterboxes.

Up the stairs I pass the sad bereaved family and through my door. Alas! The Estate agent's here again showing people round. They have taken position in all corners of the flat. So one slab of bread slathered in Stracchino will have to wait!

FEBRUARY 9th

As I stroll along busy Viale Japigia, a girl is standing near the shops. All dressed up, she looks repeatedly at her watch. Clearly waiting for someone, I sense all the anticipation of youth. It's surely a date. I imagine she's spent a long time getting ready for she's a perfect picture with those heels, that are there to be admired, rather than walked in. When I return an hour later, she's still there, but by now she seems beset by nerves.

I start to feel really sorry for her, but then a car pulls up and out of it a handsome young man with arrogant air and sunglasses perched on dark glossed hair. He seems oblivious to her suffering and soon a brief argument ensues. The young man turns back to his car and drives off at high speed. The girl struts off tossing her locks but with a tear in her eye. Romance transcends all cultures and crosses all paths. I wonder if they kiss and make up or that was the end I witnessed. I see the same girl later on that day with another girl. She looks subdued and I surmise that young love's dream didn't quite materialise.

Sometimes what you see here surprises, nonetheless. I recall one day in the centre just near La Banca di Napoli seeing a couple in their 40s who appeared full of venom towards each other, the woman then striking her man across his face. Yet five minutes later, they could be seen holding hands, laughing and discussing architecture.

Man's inhumanity to man. Would the hands that created this building or that ever have imagined such a scene?

I am tired today. Tired of walls and stone and concrete. I feel hemmed in by it all. Even the

token greenery on people's balconies doesn't assuage my sense of landlocked. We need the sea and the river and lake. We need the trees and meadows and hills. We need mountains and valleys. We need space.

We don't need yet more stone.

FEBRUARY 10th

As I sit on my bed writing up lesson plans and marking, there is a sharp knock on my door. In walk an expensively dressed and rotund lady carrying a tiny shivering dog; her dodgy looking husband; their two spoilt daughters; a screaming bambino and a plasterer with shady eyes. Following on are the landlord, his wife, and their friend, not forgetting the estate agent. My room is a little unkempt; myself even more so, so I scrabble around for my dignity as the rotund lady picks up this and that, the landlady's wife tidying as she goes. The plasterer has all his stuff with him to advance a little job on my balcony. I use the word 'my' loosely, you understand.

Trying to focus on my lesson prep becomes entirely fruitless, so I leave them all to scrutinize my room and all its worldly goods and with my British reserve scurry away sharpish. You never know who you're dealing with on these shores, so it's best to err on the side of caution. Leaving the flat never felt so good so I trip down the stairs and remember Natalie's words 'they arrive around 12 and any time up to 8'.and so I will fill my time until my lessons and then return. I take a long walk to the Duomo and find the streets busy and chaotic. The street sellers look on hopefully but I'm without change. The Duomo cafe will be my refuge for a while. Here I set about reading 'La Stampa';

'La Repubblica'; 'La Gazzetta del Mezzogiorno' and some girly magazine whilst slurping a Spremuta d'Arancia. They make good orange juice and have it in the bag. An hour has passed and so I mooch around the tourist office. I've always 'had a thing' about postcards so drink in each one; some of Lecce, others nearby parts but all present in glorious technicolour with aesthetic panache. The turquoise skies and warm-toned hues of Baroque beckon the summer to come.

Crossing the giant square to the Duomo, I enjoy the February sunshine, noting the brightness somewhat spiritual. On entering the Duomo, a warm darkness surrounds whilst aureate decorations cast their light in the sombre atmosphere. I sit awhile just soaking in this tranquil ambience, enjoying the holy and the peace.

Strolling along Via Vittorio Emanuelle and the over-priced tourist shops, I reach the taxi rank and News stand. People scurry hither and thither, a rainbow of colours adorning ancient stones.

Small dogs sit neatly in arms or trot fetchingly behind their glamorous owners. Everyone has a purpose today and tourists are thin on the ground. I would nip into the rustic pizzeria for Penne all'Arrabbiata but don't have many Euros so plump for a side-street bar. I always like to find a good one and this bar is a pleasant surprise. My cappuccino has just the right amount of froth and coffee, a soupcon of cocoa sprinkled atop. I people watch. A gaggle of carabinieri wander by with an air of importance. They are at work, but somehow I feel they are not on the case. A middle-aged man passes with his winsome wife whilst a sucked cheeked youth screeches by on his Vespa. All the while, the golden stones watch and glow in the February sun; a smell of Amaretto wafts from a nearby table and two signore chat animatedly about their lives. One sad-eyed cat miaows past and schloops down an alley. A street seller approaches and plies his wares. Comfort and poverty coexist, uneasily defining this place.

Wandering back, I return to my flat earlier than expected, but glad to find it empty. I now have that sense of unease as to when the invasion will return, but in the meantime, re-settle into my womb and fall asleep until the alarm jangles me to my lessons.

FEBRUARY 11th

It's Friday night and I'm staying at the President Hotel. A plate of Zeppole, before I climb into a much desired bath.

What a week it's been! My head is forever glued to a page.

A slight headache in the dusk, so a few drops of Lavender puts me right as the vapours rise.

Then I sit and watch Italian TV with kiddie programmeson and listen awhile to clear dulcet tones.

It reminds me of those early days in Carol Forster's life; the ones spent 'Watching with Mother'; when the flower unfolded to show this black and white story or that.
All fascinating.

Andy Pandy in his pyjamas and the tone of the narrator or The Woodentops – all strange and woody with the spotty dog. I recall I loved Pogles Wood though I don't remember much of it and of course Bill & Ben the Flowerpot Men with their strange burblings. Even at that age I found little Weed utterly irritating but two thumps of the gardener's boots, would elicit the required response. Anxiety! Along with glimpses of adult programmes, like The Prisoner or in betweeners such as The Adams Family, it seemed a strange yet interesting world that I'd entered those few years before.

Then the Clangers - the musical notes and the soup dragon. How alien yet riveting!.

Appropriately watching Italian TV and with a mouthful of Zeppola, I feel quite child-like

today. In soft pyjamas with a setting sun, I'm linked to my past through the gaudy scenes

of a few characters doing what they do – though in Italian of course. 'Watch with

Mother' as I recall had a female narrator who'd take you from mood to mood. Then '

Tales of the Riverbank' for some reason appealed less than it ought. Perhaps an early

dislike for animal exploitation, once felt so keenly at a children's circus party.

How I felt for those poor animals. Only five, but even so. Empathy, begins quite young.

For some.

The President's waiter raps on the door. More Zeppole he enquires? Of course not, I

laugh, or I'll get as fat as a winter turkey. But the Camomile goes down well and I begin

to truly relax. In a twilight doze, I think of those early times again, from Chimney Sweep

to coal house and those fascinating shops - the kerching of the cash till, all typewriter and

ping; the large bank notes and mother's words, assistants all polite. Then sixties clothes

and music in some faint whitewashed dream; red telephone boxes and bus poles and the

satchelled bus conductors. The smoky cafes and the orange juice all fish tanked by a

whooshing Horlicks machine. Reconstituted scrambled egg in a hospital stay; a

throwback from the war, I guess. All sweet memories, so riveting to a child, apart the

latter. Those early days in one's life when all is new and seen afresh. And mother's egg

nog in a yellow cup, last thing at night, after picture stories, or the nursery rhyme book

that held me transfixed and the book with a whale that was taken from its family and kept

in a tank on a ship. I cried each and every time. Or 'I'm going fishing with Alex'. Even

Janet and John. So, so long ago. A couple are shouting in the courtyard below, pulling me up sharp to the present;

Italian voices in the corridor. The other guests I feel are rooted to the here and now.

FEBRUARY 12th

I have a bit of free time today to visit Brindisi. I've seen it on the approach in the form of one tiny airport. An airport so tiny as to resemble my front room, except that I spotted the Mayor of Lecce there at Christmas.

I've decided to go the extra mile and see the town itself.

 I seem to only know it from the transport hubs, having also been to its port.

And so it was that I set off on a train to Brindisi, perhaps a little nervous as I don't know the place at all.

To quote myself from a column I wrote, ' Brindisi, much like 'Dante's Inferno', is the portal to many places. Historically a much used passageway, when the port became the main crossing point between East and West, as well as a route for pilgrims, it is used these days by holidaymakers and criminals alike'.

I rather like Brindisi with its fine passeggiata by the sea and vibrant atmosphere. Italso has an interesting link with Lecce. At one time there were two columns to mark the end of the Appian way which was the main road between Rome and the south of Italy.

However, when Leccese patron saint, Oronzo, apparently 'cured the plague, one of the columns was given to Lecce and placed in its main piazza where it stands to this day.

It has a quaint atmosphere with washing hung from balconies while Vespas whizz the place, all 1950s nostalgia.

I spent a good part of a day there perusing the town before heading back to Lecce yet noticed that wherever I roam, there is something special about arriving at the grand Lecce station with its class and old-fashioned time worn appeal.

The town's main draw, however, lies in its inhabitants.   They are unique and fine, apart from those that have other motives, who shall remain nameless.

FEBRUARY 15th

Now it's the norm. I get up increasingly early to ensure being decent when 'they' arrive. Sometimes I return to bed fully clothed, key in lock, with one eye open and one eye closed.

Natalie is grumbling in the kitchen. Anna's gone away for a few days so I repair to Davide's newsagents to do my photocopying. His shop fascinates me. At first like any other with it s array of illustrated magazines but then see behind, the guns and weaponry. To the right see children's toys and behind motorized aeroplanes. See all this and more, then wonder ...

I chat with him about the weather and observe his anxious brow. Two callous looking youths enter and demand to see the guns. Davide obliges. I feel uneasy. It's strange, this place. Just strange. I leave and will return.

Outside I hear a strange chirping. Two tiny babies have fallen from their nest. A big bruiser talks nearby on his mobile then turns to help. Concealing my surprise, he enters a shop and returns with a box. The big macho men all gather around to save the birds. I am quite amazed and touched, though a cynical moment punctuates my thoughts. I don't know why. The birds have been taken away. I hope they're ok ...

Wandering to the launderette with the whirring and whooshing of ancient machines; the prehistoric irons and engulfing smells, I go. My washing ready and given always with a tender hand. Every item is pressed to perfection. The warm sweet smell of its laundering emanates from beneath narrow sheets of tissued paper; each lovingly piled on another. The laundry ladies are there as they always are, have always been there and probably always will. I wonder if they know Davide and his newsagent weaponry shop. He's been there for many a decade too and before that his father. I know as I've seen the large black and white photo of papa Davide taken in front of the shop back in the '50s. The warm, fragrant parcel of clothes accompanies me to my flat and I put them away in drawers and try to reach the strange clothes hangers that reside a mile high in the wardrobe. Part of this fascinating piece of furniture is near the ceiling in fact, so that all the hanging parts are way beyond reach. I stare up with a certain amount of incredulity. Sometimes you just want practical!

FEBRUARY 21st

An extraordinary moment happened today. A newspaper is interested in my writing and are considering giving me a weekly column! I couldn't be happier about this as I so enjoy putting pen to paper. There is an extra prang to my step as I wend my way to school. That is until I espy 'He who is harmless but....'. Harb. He doesn't entirely seem so, but I relent and carry on regardless. I start to wonder about things and how it could be if there was some possibility to join forces with my Film Director student. He's busy creating movies and adverts and quite a creative force. After attending his casting day for 'La Zona Avvelenata' I can see there are possibilities. Perhaps we can find a way to work together.

Suddenly, quite out of the blue, my ancient admirer Ernesto appears mistaking the rosy glow on my face to be somehow related to him. He ups a gear and invites me to dinner. I need to tactfully remind him that I am wed, and happily so. His response, a little surprised and disappointed, even though he has known this for months. The old Casanova believes he still has it in the bag.

I drink my Cappuccio extra fast for I have something to do. I need a photo for my newspaper

column and it must have the relevant backdrop, so I enlist a couple of students to be photographer for the day and we meet at the corner bar and discuss locations. How about the Duomo, asks one. A possibility of course but I'd rather just explore until we find the right spot. I have a second cappuccino whilst discussing this important task, which I later regret. With a heart beating out of control -not least with the excitement of it all - we head along the Trinchese into town. I laugh gaily to myself when one photo shot requires moving on a bunch of Carabinieri. They comply, to my utter surprise. Absurdly, it becomes the one that is often used on my columns.

The photos are done and sent to the newspaper so all is set for my column launch next month.

I cannot count the days until that moment comes.

It brings to mind a poem I once wrote about Autumn and how I captured the sense of nostalgia and sadness that goes with. You may wonder why this would be, but it is merely the same emotion; one of pride in creative pursuits.

The rains start so I take refuge inside a warm bar and drop my small doily onto the floor; the one that rests my cup. The bar staff look alarmed, but maybe more because already tense.

I need a computer, but negotiating the rivers that have now formed is tricky.

And so, like the Leccese, I wait and wait and wait, until the water quietens and starts to subside, before making my way to the shop. I quickly email the newspaper to let them know how I feel. I am so happy and I want them to know I have many tales to tell. The response is fast and they, in turn, wish to 'interview' me, and so it is that I do an email interview about my life. Sometimes, as I type, unwholesome people enter the place and I sense some kind of danger but I ignore. Ignore. Always ignore.

FEBRUARY 22nd

The time has arrived for another trip to the hairdresser's.

Opening the door leads to conflicting perfumed aromas, almost to the point of suffocation, so I gasp a little before being lead to my chair by a brisk and harried hairdresser, who has each strand of his own to aesthetically pleasing perfection.

Suddenly I feel a yanking sensation as a brush is pulled through my hair and my head is put this way and that whilst Lorenzo decides my fate. Even before I can request a simple fringe cut, Lorenzo's a-chopping and a-smoothing my locks, like a wild beast that needs taming. Incredibly fast and clearly warming to his theme, he starts work on his 'masterpiece' of asymmetrical style. I'm uncomfortable with this but somehow my enfeebled tones are drowned out by the

cacophony of sound around me. A radio blares out Italian pop songs whilst regulars chat across the floor. The atmosphere is warm but busy with a million heads to foil and sort, all of them discerning ones belonging to demanding bodies. As each new arrival appears, Lorenzo and his team draw them like a black hole. Once sucked into the vortex you will never be the same again. You will be despatched like a Christmas parcel, all corners in place .

It's quite good to get out of there, I muse. I also reflect that my bank balance would be better for a number 1, though vanity gets in the way. All in all, with a strange 'work of art' on my head, that feels decidedly un-me, I bump into a student. He is polite and compliments the sculpture that was once my hair, but now I am back to the flat and Anna is there. We sit awhile drinking tea and she fills in the gaps about the flat. Natalie is moving out that very night, so tired of constant intrusions whilst Anna's to move the following week. She suggests I go too but I've already decided to sit it out as I'm only here till June. She explains how their lives have been disrupted for months. Without warning groups have entered and gone into their rooms with entitlement. I am aghast and sympathise. How can anyone live like this for a prolonged period? What will Natalie do, I ask? She'll go to her home city Naples for a while and stay with her widowed mother. Natalie is in her room and there is much activity. I surmise she's packing but on the surface of things, she's not.

All is edgy and unclear.

FEBRUARY 25th

As if my conversation with Anna didn't happen, Natalie's still here and denies her return to Naples.

Instead she's swooshing and whooshing the kitchen broom then standing on her balcony smoking.

She seems relaxed and happy but I sense unease beneath. Currently out of work, she's struggling, so her brash manner belies fear and apprehension.

Treading the pavements to work, I am accosted by my ancient admirer who descends on me like a vulture to the carrion. The folk in the butcher's smile, amused by my ordeal, as lovesick E follows me into the bar. A cappuccino sits on the table by a tiny sugar pot; steam rising into coils.

Suddenly a stranger appears in the bar with two women. They all look incredibly mean somehow; something in the eyes. The barista has a blank expression. Inscrutable. She neither displays discomfort nor joy, then a large group of nuns appear. All clad in black, they enter like rowdy schoolgirls on a day out. I am a little surprised by this light-hearted group and how carefree they seem, yet I observe through the corner of my eye, that they have something which eludes all other occupants of the bar. They are truly happy and it shows. So here we find the holy and the sinful. Italy all over.

The hard man and his women soon leave and hop into his car. Of course, it is flash and speeds off bank robbery-like. I wonder if he's happy and decide he isn't; perhaps a little too resident in his ego to know what happiness truly is. Ernesto, my ancient admirer, has a glint in his eye and is enjoying the hustle and bustle. The giant walks by, delusional as usual, muttering to himself and carrying a toy. I wonder if he's happy? I decide he is, because ignorance protects you from stark realities. He tries to lift a bin outside but fails. Perhaps it's his first taste of unhappiness after all.

FEBRUARY 27th

It's 8am and strangely quiet. I normally hear Natalie in the bathroom swishing the waters or adjusting her stuff. A little sleepy from a late night, I wander into the kitchen and using my magic lighter, turn on the gas. A small pan bubbles and I'm for a tea. The silence continues and I observe an empty bathroom. This is strange as it is never empty when Natalie's around and usually full of her paraphernalia. Her door is tightly locked with only a faint residual smell of tobacco and coffee. I've decided to visit the market today for a few plants. My balcony looks tired and empty. It's nearly spring; a thought I hug to myself. I trip trop down the four flights like a pony. A beautiful sunny day, this delights me as I feel a budding warmth on my skin. Walking briskly towards Piazza Mazzini, it's already full of the red-capped farm hands waiting for their pick up. An assortment of one-offs are hanging around too. Most don't. A Romany gypsy is begging in front of a large fashion house.   The market is young, so I go to a bar for my morning cappuccino. A red chequered tablecloth is placed, just so. My cappuccino sits in a white cup with delicate red writing that says dolce vita. Indeed it is! Sometimes. The bar staff are busy already serving their regulars a Cornetto here, Espresso there. The warm, yeasty smell of Cornetto seduces and so I tuck into the jammy delicacy then try to wipe the sugary stickiness from my mouth with a small napkin. It is hard to do this easily and I feel embarrassed when a gloop of jam falls to table. In England, it would be ignored, but here it is the greatest crime.

Che brutta figura!

I manage to snab it and put it on the doily that frills my plate. Suffice to say, I am relieved.

The market is now fully awake and a swathe of colour passes line of vision as stall upon stall display their wares. Mainly clothes and handbags hung on rails and guarded by watchful stall-holders, but the odd surprise. A Chinese stall sells all things electrical and I have to ponder awhile as to my needs. Then on to the plants and trees, that bedeck and draw like bee to flower. I stand for a while, admiring the view and try to disembody the voice that is prompting me to buy this or that. A second voice is calling me from the next stall. I pretend not to hear and focus on my purpose. What is my purpose? I mean my true one. I think to mark up my world; my crazy, topsy turvy world with shifting sands and changing faces. Plant in arms, by Piazza Mazzini, I'm irritable at the heavy pot and flailing leaves of the plant and yet I already love my new floral baby. It will have pride of place on my balcony. Arriving 'home' and entering the flat, after a rare succumbing to the lift, I am struck again by the silence.

Natalie's door is still locked and I begin to wonder. Then Anna appears. She did a midnight flit it seems. I heard nothing. How can you sleep through suitcase and box, wardrobe and stilettos on marble, without waking up. Easily it seems. Easily.

FEBRUARY 28th

I awake to hear the scrattlings of an early bird, then realise from harsh tones that the landlord's arrived He is angry with Anna and then with me, for not noticing the grand flitting of Natalie. We are a bit stumped for words, for we do not feel it our business as to whether Natalie has a flutter or flitters away. It is for Natalie to know and landlord to find out. The day continues on a sombre note but is surprisingly calm and peaceful. I have the new found pleasure of a bathroom to myself, for Anna if often away. I no longer feel a sense of urgency when i do my ablutions or have to steer a path through Natalie's stuff. Poor Natalie.

However, the evening takes an unexpected turn. One of my students – a film-maker – needs an English translator for his latest production and asks me so the night sees me chewing a pen, dictionary in hand, as I try to decipher each Italian morsel from my trusty mobile phone, as I'm without a laptop here, yet this the kind of work you need time and space for.

To my joy, some comes easily and I warm to the task. In fact, I love it ! Sleeping very little that night I chew over whether one or verb or another will suitably fit and give correct sense. I look long and hard at unfamiliar words and reflect on the gist of it bit by bit.

By 3 am I am satisfied and fall deeply asleep. My alarm some three hours later sees me pondering more but with thundering headache in tow. I nonetheless spring into Davide's and type it up with piano fingers, excitement not overriding the headache He will be pleased that it's done so quickly.

Like a cat that's been delivered the cream, I am a little pleased with myself. My confidence is up a notch and I notice that I'm smiling a more today. Even a grumpy shop-keeper catches on as my joy becomes infectious. I feel useful and even important. I feel interesting, charming and clever. Oh what a good feeling to be proud of yourself. I deserve a treat, so enter the corner bar – that is the posh one with a million pastries. I will have my squidgy Cornetto – the great big fat one – and I will not care if the jam splodges for I will be proud of myself in spite of such petty calamities..

CHAPTER SIX - MARCH

MARCH 1st

Light seeps through the slats in my blinds shedding luminous fingers of warmth across my room. I dance round it. Picture this. One pair of pyjamas with some hiking socks, leaping here and there, and then the post exercise rattling of a pan.

I have no idea why, but a memory of long ago creeps into my thoughts, as I leap around, way before the days of Lecce all 2014. It was the year of Decimilisation.

1971.

An Irish holiday. Pony trekking; long before the days of Health & Safety.

As I recall, an old man with wizened face and cynical eyes cracked a whip on the stony ground. Thwack! My father, brother and self had been plonked unceremoniously on three hapless ponies whose name or nature we knew not nor did we know how to control the beasts. Novices, all three. There was no leader nor lesson. The three, mechanically moved out of one scratty yard, along a busy road, then dutifully turned into country lane. My father's decided to munch choice weeds at the lane side. My brother's did its own thing and mine fancied someone's garden. To be more precise, it fancied the bush in someone's garden. The animal was determined and in it went. There seated on the grass was a family picnic. Embarrassment is not the word. The resigned folk seemed familiar with this routine, and so it was that a young girl led her pony back to the scratty old yard, along with her father and brother. The old man with a whip took them back with nonchalance, and the poor ponies returned to their fold. An insane thing back then, to pony trek sans experience nor wit.

The seeping light's infectious and so I head out and round past the shop with no apparent wares and the Farmacia; the extortionate dry-cleaners and the corner hair salon. I see no ponies now, only ghostly ones. I do see the landlord and his wife in their clothes shop and the inscrutable man; the one who wears expensive stuff and has superiority etched on his forehead. He's been suctioned through an electronic fence behind the defences of his car and seems important. Maybe.

I head for the little shop that sells the cheeses amongst other things. Stracchino smiles up at me, but today I'm for the Pecorino. I'm given a slab of the crumbly speckled variety, which I've never had before. It looks ancient, and probably is. The busy assistant folds it in waxy paper and puts it my way. After this, Beatola. There is something about the Italian vegetable that renders it better. The assistant speaks a little English. She tells me that she once worked in London but left her job to return, now regretted. I empathise. We've all been there. I try to give her hope, but she looks a little sad. I have a difficult class soon which presents a 'Bizzie Lizze and Little Mo' moment. How I long to touch the flower that will alter my perspective on the day. I want it over. Freedom. It's all somewhat a means to an end. Glamorous Francesca smiles broadly as I leave the school. I have my teenagers later and they are fun. How we laugh! Maybe we shouldn't. I'm the same age as them, in my head. How do you make the Past Continuous funny? We did! We achieved it. Role-play. Hilarious. Not as amusing as my Intermediates however. They are all over 40 and twice as much fun. If you could die laughing, I almost met my maker.

It's posh takeaway time. I hope to God that Harb's not about (He's alright really but...)

He was the last time I went in, but I am blessed as no multiple murderers seem present.

They are the height of genteel in here.

'Buongiorno Signora. Come sta?'

How am I? To be clear, quite hungered, especially on looking at the plump polpi in its lemon parsley sauce and the roast potatoes all coated in olive oil.

I'm just fine.

So, past the corner bar with the bird-like old lady; the fish shop; the tea shop and launderette ladies. A quick wave to those whose brows are damp. A stroll past Acqua e Sapone with it s dazzling selection of all things perfumed; the mini supermarket and ubiquitous beggar; the gift shop with cunning smiler; the perfume shop and post office. Nearly there. The six-laned road. The traffic light's not working today. They never do, even when they're working. And then it's the ancient admirer doing what he does best – admiring.

He hasn't seen me yet so I do that 'make self invisible' thing that comes in useful from time to time.

I long for my Bizzie Lizzie flower. Too late! He's seen me. With a hastening pace, he, I and Bizzie Lizzie try to cross the darn road. Now try a conversation whilst preventing certain mortality. Not only this, but the insecure paving stones look as if for a sink-hole. Then what use would this delicious Polpi meal be? It's altogether dodgy here; there are other reasons too..

But Ernesto decides it's time to show me how to part traffic.

'Signora, put your arm cosi. They will stop for you. They will stop because you have blue eyes!' He croons so now I experience a road crossing lesson combined with amorous approach.

Beam me up Scottie.

Eventually I am across and my Polpi still await so like parting Velcro from shoe, I slip away from Ernesto's ardent attentions to my apartment.

The juices of lemon and oiled parsley absorb into bread with the squares of Pecorino prove a delicious meal.

And all before Siesta time.

MARCH 2nd

It's one of those 'wading through treacle' days. I have a mountain of stuff to mark and deadlines to meet. I philosophize that I'll get through it but it's all happening today. The boiler's stopped; another electricity bill's arrived and so has my recurrent headache. On the positive side, I have a teaching session set up in Barletta soon so will be heading up there again. I decide to pre-book my train – perhaps an excuse to visit the plumptious delicatessen near the booking office, so off I trot, camera in bag. I also want more Lecce shots. I'm jealous of the postcard photographers. I want that knack. Firstly, I take a shot of Piazza Mazzini then another of Via Umberto featuring the postcard display, then finally I'm lured into a bar for a cappuccino. As I stir it with elongated spoon, I feel in sunny spirits absorbing the day's atmosphere.

It's already March and I'm only here till June. A shot of Alvini's then one of the photogenic Patisseria by Piazza Oronzo. It's cool to have a camera in such a place. Screech. Someone just crashed. Dazed but alright. Walking wounded. People gather. It seems to evaporate as fast as it came. The victim climbs back on his Vespa and buzzes off unfazed. How can a spot cream be so expensive I wonder at the shop window price. Shocking ! Not so shocking as the bedding place though. Sell your worldly goods and some for a simple duvet. The delicatessen. In here you see the plump olives and baby artichokes in pleasing pots by a million cheeses, all designed to make you drool. The cheese tester in place, a small metallic scoop, should you dither. Squidgy Gorgonzola sits lazily in waxed paper whilst a large Emmental takes pride of place. Pecorino. Parmiggiano. It's all too beautiful. I won't even use the S word today – it's understood. Squidgy as it should be though.

Hams and herbs hang from the ceiling whilst scarlet sun ripened tomatoes call to you from their bowl. And then the bread. The round and the small, the loaves and Panini. The yeasty smell lures whilst large gleaming apples wink at you. And for the seafood there on display – the polpi, the herbed fish and squid rings. Hungry is not the word as I um and ah over each tasty morsel. The shop assistant looks bored and I reflect on such nonchalance when faced with all this bounty..

Then I remember my original reason.

A train ticket pre-booked. Of course it's no competition really. A swodge of Stracchino, a splodge of Gorgonzola, a rustic loaf then a few olives in a small sealed container will complete a perfect plate.

And then for the tourist office. In sit two laconic guys, casually attired for Italy. One is also engaging in textual chat via his shiny silver mobile whilst the other engages me with ticket prices. We settle and he operates the whirring printer at a push then deftly folds the ticket snug into a pocket envelope. Ticket in bag and food complete, I head for home and marvel at the sights and sounds of this extraordinary city. It's very calm on the surface,though this belies an underlying darker side. I go past the weird Celtic restaurant that never opens and the Bingo then past the street vendors, pooches and Dok; past the 'one-offs' in Piazza Mazzini; past the fat man and his mirror-image son; past the lovers, the book-shop, Davide's newsagents. Home.

MARCH 3rd

I find myself, once again, without tea. It reminds me of those dreadful times, back in the day, when I lived in Bologna and all I could find was the wet sock variety. The waiters in cafes would give me the stuff as a treat too. 'Ah sei Inglese. Inglesina. Per te'. How I tried to sip slowly, the insipid liquor so as not to offend.

Things have improved, in that department, but sometimes you just want your English Breakfast Tea like the English supermarket variety.

I remember the first time I had tea. It was like graduating. I was given a very weak and milky one with two teaspoons of sugar. At first, not the biggest fan until I learnt to ditch the sugar. Later years saw a stronger brew until literal addiction. It s fair to say, we all are. Addicts. To take away one's tea is a cruel thing.

Beyond tea, there is a time of day for each drink. Camomile before bed or a Redbush. Tea first thing and then a coffee to galvanize and stimulate you. I never understood the 'don't like tea' people. It seems such a loss. So tragic.

I scurry round to Dok, and give a two euro coin to the homeless fellow at the entrance. I once asked him where he was from and he gave a vague reply so I'm none the wiser. I'm not sure he knew either. I asked him why he was here and he replied 'Life'. Yeah. That old chestnut. Life. It gets us in strange places doing strange things. It moves us around from pillar to post, then up and down and all around.

There they are. The red boxes of tea. Thank goodness. I can last a day without it but no longer and tomorrow's no good.

There is also the little shop near the school. They are super efficient in there. Nice. Polite. I always feel I'm intruding on their business, but I need tea. They have lots of it actually. Many different varieties all boxed in multi colours and sometimes even EBT. Tea became a bonding thing with my mother too. I'd make one for her as a gesture. A way to say I loved her. We weren't a demonstrative family. Well I was. I was probably hysterical in fact. I'd either do that or play her my Barry White or Gilbert records. She loved that. Later on I was into Soul. Everything has its time.

The lady in the tea shop waves to me ironically as I make my way to school. Bin lifter s about again. So is the tiny bird-like lady who seems to have strange things going on in her life. It's nothing to do with the bullet holes in another bar wall, she assures me and the other teachers. So that's alright then! I've got used to hearing or reading about the odd wee bomb here and there. Anyway, onto happier things, like tea.

There is now a warmth on the skin that is perceptible, even in the shade. The locals are too busy to notice but the pasty English teachers such as myself do. I have another problem. My mobile battery has conked out and is doing strange leaky things. I explain this to my students and they tell me that it's dangerous and advise me where to go. And so I risk life and limb crossing those roads and weaving through Vespas to the Electrical shop. No battery that fits, of course. It's never that easy. The day wears on and I have an idea. One of my students works for the Carabinieri. She's a nice Carabiniere and called Mariella. Extremely helpful she has tried several times to sort things out for me and advised me of a shop near Piazza Mazzini; a kind of physical representation of PMT as I remember it. You feel anxious but ok really. You know it'll pass. There are always a lot of strange people hanging around amidst the normal ones there. Anyway, as I search for the shop, and eventually find it I see a young street vendor who asks me what I'm looking for, I explain and he takes me to the very shop. Kind. I offer him a Euro but he refuses. Dignity in adversity.

These moments. Precious.

To my joy, they have the battery. The very one. However, I receive a telling off by the shop assistant for carrying the loaded gun that is a faulty one around with me. Che brutta! I am horrified but tired so duly pop in the goodie and remove the baddie.

I feel like a born again. Dante's Inferno. A bit of hell; purgatory being the moment of realisation and then reaching heaven with the goods.

I long for a TV, almost as much as I once wanted a pony. My mother responded with 'Agh love, it won't fit in the back garden' and that was that. I eye one up enviously through a shop window. Maybe, but I have so many other things to consider first. How about starting with the rent, the phone bill and food, then continuing with flights home and back. TEFL teaching is not all Rockerfeller, so I do my best until I see a wodge of exquisite proportions in a shop window on the way back. The Stracchino wodge.

I have one hope – that the packaging of a Stracchino square of squidgy squodginess is never changed. The ice-cream styled packet is part of its success. The unveiling and satisfying corners of the squat envelope. Do not put it in a box. Ever.

MARCH 4th

My friend Maria has offered to take me up to the Gargano region for the weekend. Of course this is really a summer destination, but even out of season, I sense its appeal.

I first came here many years ago. 1989 it was. A n extremely hot June Saturday and the beach side cafes were thronged with Italians enjoying their lunch. I recall the Insalata alla Marinara even now and the gloop of an Espresso to follow. We sunbathed on the beach back then, my friends and I, enjoying the rays and the ambience. I recall the pristine sea, as limpid and clear as you can imagine. The sands were palest gold, the heat intense. I even got a little sunburnt that day. So as we drive up on this day to the area, I remembered all this with a wistful eye.

It was very quiet when we arrived though not dead. Most of the hotels, however, were firmly shut for the winter so, instead of staying there we just meandered about Vieste and then visited Peschici -both gorgeous spots in the Gargano national park.

Maria had only been here once before too so we both looked upon the experience with fresh eyes.

It felt a little sad, out of season, but nonetheless, appealed to my sense of space and light as I looked out at the gentle lapping shore.

A jangly phone call knocked us from our reverie and meant an early return to Lecce. A family matter. It was a long but nonetheless pleasant drive back, as we reminisced about the past and our lives lived before now. When I returned to my flat, I found the welcome sight of some Gorgonzola from the day before which placed itself nicely on a hunk of bread and was devoured along with a Camomile tea. I needed it somehow. The week had been long and I was for a long rest.

MARCH 5th

A bath in the oval tub and some milk was all I required tonight. The day has been stressful. Some old girl had died and all the comings and goings kept me awake. I'd read and re-read the book; the one bought from the African about his journey here. It didn't mention when. But then at 3 am, that ghostly hour, I heard a noise like someone gasping for breath then a muffled voice and the rapping on a door. Light on, and heart in mouth, I peered through the eye-hole. Pitch. Nothing and noone perceptible. All quiet again. There was a chill that night, all supernatural. I re-read the book to lighten up. Not a sound. No sound. Eerie, until the snoring from next door. All mundane and right again. I saw a ghost once. I'm sure I did. 1980 it was. My friend Christine's old cottage. 17th Century with its low ceilings. Downstairs we slept. Woke up. There it was. A dark apparition of someone, something leaning towards the old oak table, some inches above ground level. I remember darting underneath the covers as if to cancel out. Some believed it, others not. Who knows. I also saw another thing. Once. Fifteen I was. I think they call it Astral projection. The bright white form of a sleeping girl rising from her body. I was in the twin bed. I saw it. Weird. Wonderful too. Peaceful. Holy even. Why I saw it, I'll never know.

At times there is a presence. I know that someone died here, just a few years ago... Sometimes mundanity is wonderful. To see the workman with his tools a tapping here and there. At other times it bores, transcending earthly concerns.

Via Oberdan. Lecce. From the corner, past the furniture shop; the posh veg one. The charming couple wave and all is well, then the hairdresser's and near the flat I once heard 'Non posso piu!' at alto volume. Past the mystery shop I stroll, and the several bars. One bar has a grumpy visitor. He grumps the place and bothers everyone. I see it whenever I pass. Grump. Grump. Grumpetty grump. What a misery he is.

It's Saturday and hardly yet so I pass the strange piazza to walk the walk along the glamoured parts. The market's open and swinging. The bar is also open. I drink a Spremuta and sit perched high like some Golden Eagle to read, 'Il Quotidiano di Lecce'. I wish I hadn't. It is a terrifying read. The murk beneath the golden stones. I cannot cope on fruit juice alone and so the Capuuccio follows on. With sugared froth it hits the spot and then I wander busy stalls, and scrutinize the Chinese one. Endless clothes stalls. Endless. Some stuff good. I buy a long navy jumper thing. It swathes me and reaches the right points on each limb. And then I'm for my favourite street; the postcard lined one, all golden. Gold in the morning and the cyclist like it. Via Umberto 1. So do the mopeds. So do I. So does the small man with a huge dog and the woman with her beau.

It's early . A local man ambles past. He's well-dressed and groomed. Typico. He's carrying a small shoulder bag and paper and looks bored. Let's re-run that. He's walking along Via Umberto 1 in the gorgeous baroque town of Lecce, in the Salento region, and he's bored? He's walking near neat cafes and balconies; the golden hues and planty pots; the Carabinieri parts and restaurants; the post-cards and the dogs. And he's bored? Of course. Familiarity and all that. He probably doesn't notice the fine Baroque of Santa Croce any more or care for the dishes made with exquisite scarlet pomodori. It's all internal really. It's all inside. He just wants to read the paper, and so he should.

As I sit, a large African girl comes my way. In brightest robes, she's selling jewellery with aggressive tones. She puts it in front of me and demands I buy. I don't want to. I feel sorry for her but no. She insists and insists again. That's a swodge of Stracchino and some bread; a Cornetto or two.

It's 10.30 and I'm not enjoying it now. Her life. What life. Existence. Struggle. Survival. Anxiety. I wonder of her story but guess it's no different, and as she finally stops pestering, I cave in and buy a bracelet. I'm like that sometimes. A dog is yapping at my ankles. No peace. Moving on through the old back streets and there's the charming ticket office and Tourist Information. Like no other, near the posh hotel. I stayed there once. Very plush. I left my window blinds open and when I woke they were flapping like some angry bird against the wall. I could see a scaffolded Santa Croce and the cute ticket office; a bank to my left. October sun. Beautiful, apart the scaffolding. But the flapping of the blinds on stone had altered those moments forever. Somehow threatening. Not welcome. Here.

I read a story once about a man who'd won the lottery. He'd had a heart attack and died straight after. That sort of thing. You can't argue with fate. So gorgeous view and flapping blinds it is.

Nearby there's an ice-cream place. Big and busy, not my scene. I do like Alvino's though. It's big and busy too.

No rules then.

Not only do you get to eat the sticky sweet of a thousand cakes,and Zeppole aplenty, you also see the old Roman amphitheatre laid before you, mid bite, like some peculiar gladiatorial moment. You can see the taxi drivers, pleased as punch. I don't know why. They're reliable and I use them now and then. One has long hair. It reminds me of another time; perhaps my 74 trip to Rimini. We'd stayed in a hotel with a diamond pool.

Fruit for desert. Hard fruit, I recall. I liked the place though. Loved it. Who wouldn't? I recall Maria Muldaur playing on a radio, 'Midnight at the Oasis'. Perfect for the July warmth and August greened sea; the parasols and tat. Summer Breeze by the Isleys would have completed the picture, but it wasn't playing at the time.

The grand streets are all here, in the centre. The dog sleeps outside its shop. It is its shop; I see it in his eyes. And then across the other side one sells all things chocolate. Too much of anything can put you off. It does. I can't explain why Alvino's is different. I don't know.

No rules.

I gave ten Euros to a street vendor here one day back in October. No reason. Upbeat mood probably, but bought nothing. He looked amazed, as if I'd given him the elixir of life. I looked at him again. I think on drugs. His eyes were somewhere else.Shame. Real shame. Both ways. Two Carabinieri hovered by. Protectively. The gullible tourist, or so they likely thought. What about the man? He was the picture of our shame. He had nothing. Nothing at all save a few soiled clothes and my ten Euros.. He was street dead. It touched me. They all do. Sad . Sorry. And then there's the kiosk with all its wares: Newspapers,Magazines, Small toys. A young child perches beside the vendor. All fine with them. Happy enough.

The cafe I enter is busy. Too much. Chicken panino. Fine idea but not fine. It's breaded. This reminds me of fried Mars Bars. Here? Surely not. Not right. Unnecessary. Remove the breaded parts. Out . Home. Done.

MARCH 6th

I'm missing water. The taps are working but no canals, seas or rivers here. We're down south with its Mediterranean climate but what use without sea, or at least some kind. I remember once in the early days of our love, husband James and I would walk along the canal in northern England. Beautiful green fields on both sides. Cows and sheep, as expected. As we walked, we suddenly noticed a shoal of fish. Some were quite big, others small. Roach. I was spellbound as I've always loved aquatic creatures. Fry. They swam in all directions yet synchronised. My husband said later how he'd loved me for it; that child-like fascination with fish.

There's no water here. No husband either. He's in England but we're strong and will survive. As if to prove a point, a tap drips relentlessly into the sink. Water torture. It's the thing that lacks here. I know there are buses and trains. Gallipoli. Otranto. Porto Cesareo. Santa Caterina. All. But I want that here beside the sandy Baroque frills of a building and the aromatic cafes; beside the sweetmeat shops; the Zeppole and tarts.

I want the green waters of La Baia Verde. Yes. But here, not there.

Years ago I took my son to Oasis. Not the band, but the place - forest thing with wooden lodges and cycling tracks. Busy in July. He was young then. We searched in vain for Dexter the Dinosaur one year. He'd been there the year before. No can do. He'd gone. Scarpered. I tried to explain to a five year old. Difficult.

There wasn't much water there either; a man-made lake. So near to all the great northern too, yet so far.

A bit like this.

It's not just about the lack. Once seen and not forgotten. The sea at Otranto. Turquoise. Inviting. Seductive sea. Why not here? But if nothing comes from age but wisdom, I know this: Happiness is that you can acquire. Unhappiness is that you never will. Not possible so not to dwell.

Music. Again. The trumpeter is good. I heard him more when I lived on Via Oberdan. He practised every day. Religiously. Not like my recorder days with 'Little bird, I have heard' After school, when you were tired. Out they'd come. Mine smelt a woody wood. I was quite good really until you blew too heard, then you blew it. But after school when you want to unwind. No.

He can play, the trumpeter. He does it professionally, I think. I don't know who he is. And then came the violin and the guitar. Quite good, though after school still. One was on a street near the bus station. The teacher was young and gifted with talons on one hand. A room smelt of Raffia with guitars for sale. I'd wait in there, fascinated by the sights and smells of a dozen stringed instruments. Then came my lessons. Inspiring. I learnt some Spanish bits and bobs. Nice. The violin more serious. More resin of the bow. The knuckle rapping piano teacher was long gone. Dead even. She'd been ancient from the start. I'd liked the sweets at the end of lesson. I also liked the Peardrops from the corner shop all squished in greaseproof bag and twizzled round till plumply secure. Some chocolate drops and icing flecked on. It coincided with Measles. Or was it Chickenpox? The drops reminded me of same. Strange.

Then Etch-a-Sletch. Fascinating. Still would. 1960s childhood. Spiromatic was a thing. Throwing paint at paper spinning round, all Jackson Pollock as aforementioned, but Spirograph really held me in its grip. I was spellbound by the cogs and pins and then the exquisite patterns following on.

So so long ago. But not forgotten. Lovely.

Jazz becomes Lecce and yes, he's a jazz trumpeter.

For me this genre transcends all others. Genii all of them. To improvise at will is a gift beyond. I like to live my life like this. Surprises; though good of course. The bad ones are beyond the pale.

I recall, once when doing an Italian course up in Viareggio, Tuscany. 1990 to discover my class-mate to be the manager of some rock group. Deep Purple, no less. Hardly random. All neat cravatte and slicked back hair. He was well-groomed. And polite. Great fun. I loved it.

Out of context always good.

So here in Lecce, amidst the sandy stones and fine carved rock, you'll find a jazz-filled bar in the evenings. As you'd expect it's excellent. Even perfect. Saint Patrick's Jazz Club in Barletta has it in the bag. The food. The drink. The place. The Jazz... Ambience all thought out and delivered. Very popular.

Here in Lecce, I am drawn to the President. Hotel that is. It's not as grand as some, but I have stayed here several times now. They are kind. Near Viale Japigia in fact. The rooms snug and practical and evenings have been spent watching the TV here in Lecce. Watching, as I do, to improve my Italian and to relax. Why not? A bit of Montalbano and a lot of 'C'e Posta per te'. My students were embarrassed when I told them. I am not. I love it, sentimentality and all. Long lost people meet up again. There are tears each week. Hugs and tears, mine too. It all comes out –unrelated perhaps...

It beat s 'Colpo Grosso' hands down. Dreadful thought. Years ago. 1989. Breasts everywhere and some. A bit of RAI news and I'm there, watching the world go by in another form, relaxing with my Camomile; a sauce bathed pasta dish consumed. The breakfasts are generous too. All cakey, sweetmeat stuff, as you would expect. Nice. Business people sit quietly at this hour. Unusual here. No blaring TV in the Breakfast room, thankfully. Nice. Cappuccio made and poured. A perfect start. My bolt-hole. Tap needs fixing though.

MARCH 7th

I had a reverie today. Back, back, back in time. I remembered reaching for the glass cat on the chest of drawers. High up there. Perhaps age of two. I remembered a nursery visited. And then my favourite one: The pushchair. Now I was quite content in it, as I recall. I liked the sensation of pavement and road beneath the rolling wheels; my mother's pulls and tugs. All strapped in and snug, watching the world pass by. I even recall my high chair days. And high it was and wooden with plastic parts. Formica. What a smell! You'd wait for your food like a nesting chick, and then have it spooned right in. Loved it. Always loved food, apart from school milk as Russell's snot got in my view. Only five but these impressions last. It was several years before I'd drink the stuff again. Association. Poor Russell and his snot. I wonder what he's doing now? He might be famous or even dead. As long as he's discovered Kleenex. And now I'm sitting on my balcony on one stiff upright chair; the tiny table is before me and the used ashtray of a previous tenant. I'm sleepy with the midday sun and balcony views across the strange zone between two boxed palazzi, where prongy things lurk. I think they're to do with the foundations of some old building, yet resemble a Dr. Who set. They remind me of coat hangers, all wodged on a concrete bed. The boy across the way is performing his daily routines. Autistic perhaps. Probably. A maid is scurrying round then takes a break. She sits awhile and plays her phone. Some things translate. Somewhere in the distance, I hear a gun being fired. It could be any situation. Here, like a steamroller, we just smoothe our way along. I hear the words, 'Mi raccomando' once again, regular as clockwork.

MARCH 8th

Mellow clouds are lining the Leccese skies. Lemon are they and dappled with the purest blue. I'm wearing blue as well and a cream linen top. My sandals are quite high and so I totter along Viale Japigia risking certain accident. I'm for the Deutschebank and so today the odd experience of being one of those the guard must watch. Vortexed inside the banky tardis and encased. Press green for go and then I'm teleported inside. Here I am enquiring about Sterling , yet the English notes seem somewhat out of my league. The bank cashier is grumpy and perplexed. No, they don't. OK. Then the nice once comes along

'Ma ciao Signora. Si certo' Yes they do. Yes, no, in, out, shake yourself free of all doubt.

I don't know why I'm surprised. It's exactly the same each time. Grumpy no. Nice one yes. Grumpy can't be bothered to dig the paltry wee notes out. Can't say I blame him. And then they appear, all shiny and new, wrapped in a neat Italian envelope.

Thank you very much. I assume the guard is not protecting the few Sterling here as I think I've got the lot! I smile at him on my way out and even say hello, then I totter down the street, past the weird Celtic restaurant where nothing seems to take place,ever, and the 1950s Tabaccheria with its cigarette machines all wooden drawered.

Inside a harassed assistant deals with gap-toothed men. Some have gaps because of age, whilst others no excuse. They're on their Scratchcard rounds. Across the road, a garden sits behind a high-wired fence. The fence is so high that is reminiscent of a zoo. I imagine a lion roaring there, and perhaps the zoo keeper is the man I see in slippers on his front step.

Crossing roads towards the President, I see a band emerge. With instruments all encased, they're on their way somewhere or other. Stopping through. Then along this road to the strange bookshop with an eerie atmosphere; a million books. I need a good Italian dictionary and I'm shown about ten to choose from so whilst teetering on much regretted heels, I buy the one that strikes most readily to me. And then I teeter to the cheese shop for the usual. When the stationery girl next door enquires as to my choice of shoe, noticing my discomfort, I'm able to say quite comfortably a bit, fat 'Boh!', my favourite Italian word.

As I stand perched aloft, a man enters and tries to start a conversation with me.

'Lei Inglese?'

He then asks for my help. Running an Art Gallery he needs a translator for his clients. Unfortunately both our hopes are quickly dashed for the timing is all wrong. I'm glad to be asked though and was also glad to be asked by the Estate Agent for English lessons, and the girl in the corner bar. None worked out, not even the hairdresser wanting English for his children. All at the wrong time Peccato.

Tottering back to my flat, I suddenly spot Harb (He's alright really but...). He's going left so I go right; even though it's not my natural way. I notice how the people step aside and avert their glance. I saw that in a shop too. The one to be wary of hanging around. We all knew. Everyone did. Omerta.

So I glide along. You soon learn to glide in Lecce and for two reasons: One is for bella figura and the other for Omerta.

Just glide along. No need to smile inanely though. Just glide and wave to the bank guard. It is admittedly hard to do whilst wearing these damndable shoes.

MARCH 10th

The signs of spring are enticing and that sense of warmth and light pervades all corners of my being. I have lessons today but feel free and want to roam the city a little. The car that drones its engine drowns out my thoughts and I notice the occupants look less than friendly. Determined not to let this spoil my day, on I stroll along the streets to the centre whilst planning my next trip . I wish I had wings beneath my feet and could teleport wherever the whim took me. I'm suddenly struck by the beauty of it all; the flowers, placed just so, along stylish avenues. The noise of a Vespa completes my reverie into something that is all but a reality. This is the real Italy. The voices and laughter dance along with the mopeds and cars; hours of sunshine seeping through shutters. When I think back a few decades, I couldn't have conceived Lecce. How can one know that they will one day be in some far flung place with the aroma of coffee; the scent of spring; the cheeps of foreign birds; the signs of another language, all communicating to you the same thing. Your surreal moments transformed to reality. Your daydreams. Perhaps you had glimpses once – in some film or even a TV advert. Perhaps you dreamt it as a child. Maybe you always knew. But you are here. And after all those dull, grey days of younger times, wishing for excitement, even thrills when you realise your life has changed and it almost crept up on you. An old black and white film, now in vivid colour and sunkissed stones. Our dreams are us and we can become them as we look at a damp

English garden, the grey city stone. We dream and we hope. We may even realise or release that hope one day.

MARCH 11th

A cornucopia of thoughts beset me today. Busy, but little time to prepare. The night was restless and the street noises relentless. Another year of my life has passed and the time that I've spent here is but a fraction of the composite.

A nagging thought enters my head: What will the future hold and, indeed, how will it unfold? The dawning of spring has brought with it that exposed feeling; as if standing on a cliff edge against a searing wind. Today the light seems more brash than bright and the sounds intrusive rather than interesting. The long day ahead looms. I have meetings and lessons and shopping to do but after little sleep, it all seems insurmountable. I can hear voices outside my door which seem to reverberate around my room. It's a family affair. Maybe some relatives have arrived for the lonely old couple next door. As the lift isn't working, I trot down the polished steps and smile at an old lady leaving her flat. Only five days to go until my birthday. Another one. The earliest in London. The middle ones up north. A few abroad and now, again. A life. Time and so much of it. The early birthday parties with the Salmon finger buns and the three- tiered chocolate cake made by mother. The games and the party bags; the Pass-the-parcel and the Etch-a-Sletch moments. The Musical Chairs. How long ago this all seems now as I walk along Viale Japigia. The Deutschbank guard isn't there today. I wonder what he's doing. Perhaps it's his birthday too. I muse over how he must fill his thoughts whilst keeping guard. A duality of mind and purpose. Does he, perchance, think about Christmas whilst eyeing the dodgy one that approaches. I wonder if he's done a flit and is currently sipping an iced drink on some distant beach.

It's also five years now since I lost my mother. The gut wrenching grief. The incredulity. The shock. The pain and sorrow. Such terrible terrible sadness. Seeing her coffin. That's my mother in there. Beyond words. That's my mother that used to make birthday cakes and iron my clothes. That's my mother that used to pick me up from school. That's my mother. Words cannot convey.

As I walk past the post office, I hear a voice calling, 'Signora! Signora!' and look round to see one of my favourite students, Alessandra who is hot footing it to school. We talk a little in English but also Italian and discuss the problems of language learning as we approach the school. As it's still early, we decide to nip into the corner bar. 'He who is harmless....' has entered the bar and I see the inscrutable bartender's neutral expression. Through the window I see a brightening day, punctuated by thoughts of work to be done. How can I possibly face the day when all I want to do is daydream and sleep. Alessandra is a tonic so that by the time I've entered the classroom I feel somewhat prepared for the Future Tense. The day drags and so I push my way through it, all cylinders firing, until finally, finally all is complete and I can return to my flat. Life is all about balance. Without the heavy, there is no light. And so it was, I felt a certain gratitude that the relentless day had taken place; that all the headaches and annoyances had come and gone. I felt even grateful that my second lesson had been disastrous. At least, this way, I could now lie back in the deep bath filled with warm and fragrant water, hoping tomorrow would be different.

MARCH 12th

It's shiny and it's perfect and it floats, my new shirt, bought from a clothes shop on Via Trinchese for 30 Euros precisely. It's white and flutters in the breeze and wafts around as linen should. I'm near the Duomo with only one thought. Past the sculptor and the Tourist Office and the street book-seller to the Spremuta. It's in a large glass. It's so warm now and I feel dehydrated. As it cools my throat, I shiver. So refreshing. I read 'La Stampa' and 'Il Quotidiano di Lecce', I wish I hadn't. There beneath the golden celestial Baroque; the sweet smell of coffee; the sumptuous views; the ancient streets; the sunshine; the glorious architectural genius, do lie some small nuggets of criminality. Petty and so out of place in this beautiful town, this heavenly sphere. Paradise etched with darkened spots. Such a shame – as if a long beautiful road, full of beautiful souls sees one fall this way or that, off course to another place ...

I have no classes today and on my travels further afield so I'm for Gallipoli. It chugs, the train, but arrives and the pristine waters by the fishermen's nets seem alive. I cannot decide quite what I think of this place. It has a charm but with some rough corners. I find the restaurant by that beach; the one all the postcards show – and eat some garlic pasta. The warmth makes me so sleepy and after a wander, I make for a bright looking B & B and book a room. On the small bedside table sits a vase with palest yellow flowers. The room is neat and perfectly clean. White curtains blow by the shuttered window. I have a lovely view of boats and sea and cafe awnings. My room's exquisite and so cheap! I lie back on a golden hand-embroidered counterpane. Above me only the freshly painted ceiling of an old building. The wear and tear shows in the undulations. A gilded chair sits in the corner beneath an artist's sketch of the town. I sleep and dream of summers past; of primary coloured boats bobbing in some harbour; of golden sands squidging between my toes and lapping sea shallows. I dream of summer meadows sprinkled with pastel flowers. I dream of sanctuary and peace.

MARCH 16th

I wake up to my birthday and a steady flow of work. I don't dread the passing years and love the day you can call your own that tells you another year has been survived. It's my day and I will throw my arms around it in glorious gratitude and joy. I love birthdays and this is mine. I'm staying at a hotel tonight. It's in the centre of Lecce with smiling staff and polished floors. My lessons hubble along but by the end, freedom tastes sweet as I whizz along to my hotel, bag already packed. To me, the joy of hotels is the privacy and solitude that can be chosen; the buttons to press and the sheer comfort. The zoned in or out sensation of all things leisurely. The senses fine-tuned to the sensory. The eyes relaxed. The mind calmed. The belly satiated. The 'What if I press this knob or that?' The Where is the and what is it like? The bathroom; the toiletry gifts; the power shower. Oh the bath! The perfect TV and the swirling curtains. The scented pillow and the food warming clang thing. The multiple lights and the lazy remotes. The hotel slippers all plumptious and right. The bathrobe all towelly and white. This fingertip world that is eons from that ratty, gritty life where puddles get splashed on hapless pedestrians; where humanity cries and hustles and tries. Here I'm not trying. I'm just being – and it's bliss.

MARCH 23rd

The warmth on my skin is intoxicating and a vague aroma of flowers wafts my way. I cannot believe the quality of light. It's delicious and ethereal. It's holy. I see a beautiful garden and feel a spiritual flow, all loveliness and warmth. I'm hovering above the cracked pavements that suggest earthly concerns and look upwards to see a palm frond gently wafting in a gentle breeze. These days I've shed some layers and the intake of heat is increasing. I bought a simple meal today of Olives, bread, tomatoes and the squidgiest Gorgonzola that spread divinely on the yeasty wonderment and melted in my mouth. The tang of tomato complimented perfectly. My friend Maria has brought me some plump sweetened biscuits, fresh from the patisserie. Vanilla wraps itself around almonds, fruits and butter to bind into one delicious globblet. We talk awhile about life. Sometimes I have to remind myself that people who speak another language, have the same concerns as me. Silly I know. Yet somehow, in this glamorous world, you assume the mundane botherments of a lesser existence rarely register. It's not true of course and all the angsts and cares of this world are not spared. A peaceful walk at dusk dims the worries as we mooch in shops and drool at some perfect dress or other. I've forgotten all about sad light. You know that autumn ambience which I love, that tells of sorrows past; nostalgia tugs that catch your breath. Here it's been vapourised. I don't know if that's a good thing or not. Here is now and proud. It tells of nothing more and nothing less. A wrinkled brow is ironed out, as if some giant press were ready to smooth the way. The rustle of some bushes reveals a cautious cat, working into a small shrubbery. What of mice or perhaps lizards? A different menu here for puss. The evening starts to throw its mantle over the town and a slight chill takes hold. We've had a hot chocolate in a quiet bar. I am ready for the hours ahead. Primed. I notice a few bullet holes along the way. Like a beautiful painting with damaged parts, nothing is perfect. There has to be the flip side of the coin too.

MARCH 25th

Sitting in the corner bar observing the beautiful people, and feeling restless, I draw on my inner self to reach that place where I reside. My inner sanctuary. I feel the urge to go somewhere to de-Lecce-fy, and so I contact my friend Maria and arrange to do a road trip to Martina Franca.

I've never been here before but as she recommends it, I am happy to enjoy the ride and explore the unknown. Driving along the olive-groved road, watching peach and pink villas weaving Vespas, I relax into the journey, feeling the optimistic air that comes with spring. I watch the rooftop birds admiring their flights, envying their freedoms, there above the mundane world of earthly necessities, looking down on us, or perhaps simply ignoring us. The sun dances gently on the rooftops. Eventually we approach the town, so Maria finds a suitable parking slot near a large black car with rotund smoking driver. It looks as though he has a girlfriend to his left, and I sense this a secret rendezvous. We wander at gentle pace through the medieval centre with it s Baroque features. I enjoy the walk immensely and we laugh merrily linking arms in the Spring sunshine. There are some street beggars at the corner who draw us in with their eyes. We pay and feel a little subdued afterwards. The chill in the air makes me grateful for my jacket but I'm missing my hat and my husband too. The cool air rustles my hair and bothers me but I am never long from a cafe, so we find the most appealing one and enter.

Cupping our cappuccinos, we people watch awhile. Everyone looks extremely smart as they wander by, then I realise it is a large family occasion and that they are heading to a wedding. Satiated with the vittels of a panino, we wander through the Porta di Santo Stefano into Piazza Roma, where we see the Palazzo Ducale, currently a town hall. I am quite taken with the 18th century murals so we linger awhile as I ponder how works of art so often become the backdrop to modern day functionality in Italy. Approaching Piazza Plebiscito we see the Chiesa di San Martino and admire its Baroque facade. I note to myself that I am now extremely taken with Baroque architecture and a great admirer of those who created it. After all, it is now part of my everyday experience. Such an exquisite eye for aesthetics. Quite awe inspiring. I reflect on this attention to detail and wonder how long it took the architect to create .

As if in a different world, and on different time, they must have learned to switch off the pressures of the clock. So, in that beautiful image, lies the gift of unfettered time. We decide then to wander to the old town walls where I'm delighted to see views of Valle d'Itria and its fields and those conical shaped stone houses called 'Trulli'. I take some shots with my phone then realise my battery's running low, so my quest is somewhat hindered. We lunch in a nice rustic trattoria then, feeling as plumped as a winter bird, we head back to the car. Our mysterious car neighbours have vanished so we drive back towards Lecce, admiring the afternoon sunshine which rests on pink-hued palazzi. On returning to my flat, I run a bath and lie there in a sense of wonderment at this extraordinary country. It is the architecture that really takes me, transcending the humdrum world.

Sublime.

MARCH 30th

I'm meeting some friends this morning in the Duomo bar. They're to speak English and me Italian. We are a disconbobulation of verbal error with verbs misplaced and misused. But what of it? How we laugh. It reminds me of a course I did on cross-cultural miscommunication when I learnt that English requests can seem very rude to the Chinese ear. I digress.

The Leccese are so warm and their brio infectious. How subtle language is, and yet how can it matter when we are friends who have bonded. Not a jot! Mistaken insults disappear. A smile returns. A spremuta is beckons me from its generous glass – all Sicilian orange juiced citrus tones. An elderly couple sit nearby reading a newspaper in silence. I observe the perfect creasing of his trousers; the polish of his shoes. Nothing in their appearance suggests slovenly or a lack of conscious effort. Aloof, yet gentile, they sit awhile, and tolerate the babble from my table. Some tourists are in the Duomo square. They are being gathered and led like ducklings by their mother, to see the interior of the great building. With sunglasses perched and hands shielding the light, like a searching party, they seek and they shall find. All is calm and cultured. The bookshop nearby displays every morsel of the literary world. Every book a masterpiece of form. Every step is a mouthful of elegance and exquisite attention to detail. Even gaudy has finesse. We laugh. We talk. Life goes on

CHAPTER SEVEN - APRIL

APRIL 1st

April 1st and feeling suitably fool. I've arrived at school and forgotten the work. And so I head back along the road towards Viale Japigia and its six-laned thrills; risk life and limb, again, and wave to the bank guard on my return. He looks surprised for obvious reasons. Soon I am laden with books and wave again. Someone nearly gets run over. Not me, I hasten to add. They don't and that's as good as you can expect here.

And as I wander back along Via Leuca towards the school, I see a million carabinieri on their way to the church - so many, it is like a cloud of Calabrone. People step respectfully aside, and let the merry men on their way. They are indeed a merry lot and seem unaptly so as on closer inspection I realise it is a funeral. The laundry ladies tell me so. A colleague. They pile inside the church, all gleaming uniform and as they pass, the street vendors and beggars straighten up and look to the floor. The Carabinieri have no truck with them today.

On entering the school I am bedazzled by the sight of flowers all neatly arranged on the secretary's table. And then on entering my classroom, I see posters from my last kiddie lesson of spring flowers and little lambs. I smile, before putting pen to board and thus commence my lessons for the day.

The light is such that I sit awhile to watch it through the shuttered window, now open to the day. From my balcony I see Harb, who spoils the scene. The light holds me there a while and I recall it from before.

Siena it was. April. The light fell in shards across Piazza del Campo from the cafe, where I sat with a Canadian businessman. He was using me as his translator and so we'd pass from launderette to shop to cafe, and I would say the required words and he would pay. It seemed a fair deal to me.

I remember once, we sat at cafe, me with tea, and watched the children playing in the big piazza. And as the sun fell on the stones, I recall thinking that it was perhaps the most beautiful sight I'd ever seen. Everything was in its place, and even the pigeons seemed to know. And then one day, as I sat at the cafe, enjoying its view, I looked down at my sandal and there, crawling across, was a tiny brown scorpion, much like a bug. I watched in horror as it reached the outer reaches of my sandal that would then become my foot, and crossed my skin, all delicate like, with no venom at all.

It was a stange experience, that, watching the scorpion cross my foot whilst eating the most divine ice-cream from the multi choice place. Extraordinary. Then it scuttled across the stones and away.

I'd eat garlicked Spinach there. Regularly. It was delicious. The tea was less so, I recall. A limp grey affair that rendered sock.

But that was Siena by day. By night it was quite something else. Spooky. Hardly surprising given its history, but never more so than the Torre I lived in for a while in countryside nearby. 11th century it was.Eerie. My first night there, I was alone and lay relaxing in the modernised bathroom. I heard a crack and recall, a windless evening. Shutters shut. There was no wind. None at all. There were no people, none at all. And yet a candle placed middle of the kitchen table, was thrown onto the floor...

And then my clothes covered by my own hair shampoo one day, on my return. I soon realised the place was haunted and moved fast to another place.

APRIL 3rd

The zig-zagged pattern of a shop window draws my eye and makes me think somehow of childhood, playing with friend Alison without a care in the world, other than whose turn it was to use the Hopper or gather dandelions for her pet tortoise. As I enter the stationery shop near the school, the rainbowed paper and card squats neatly by myriad colouring pens and glittery parapheranalia. I gather some for my youngest students. We are on a Spring theme, and create beautiful pictures of summer meadows with ever present sun shining down on us, bestowing warmth; that life giver. Small Mario enquires whether we have spring in England and I am at a loss as to the answer. Sometimes, I offer. As I wander the streets towards the Pasticceria, I'm advancing towards my little corner of the sublime. It make a perfect cappuccino, frothed just so, and delicate little Cornetti squodged with jammy mouthfuls. I fancy this today – there seems to be a small gap in me just waiting for this.

The owner smiles benevolently and I stand sardine with the usual clientelle all in perfect order, neatly styled. As it's right next to the coolest hairdresser for miles, this whole zone is a fashion alert for those not in the know. Today I feel the part though, having perfectly matched ensemble of wardrobe. A dish of plump Sicilian lemons draws my eye there against the palest blue shop wall; a stunning backdrop to the golden pastries dashed with jammed coloured gloops and noblets of chocolate.

After this I head for the station as I'm travelling to Ostuni. I've planned it for ages and I have my pink digital ensconced in a small travelling bag. The train is brimful on its long Adriatic journey through the Puglian towns, A small child plays with a toy, without thought for the goings on around it but I arrive in Ostuni and repair to a small hotel for the night.

Delicate pale mauve flowers decorate the entrance and remind me of Lavender. An instant calm pervades and I 'm soon asleep, a belly full of cheese pasta. On waking, I'm delighted to see the beautiful gleam of those white buildings in the sunlight, so happy it's fine weather for even here can be unpredictable. Globules of light dance on the stones as people meander; some on their daily runs, whilst others to admire. It strikes me this divergence of interest and and how we overlook and stop 'seeing' when we are always in a place. I've fallen a little in love with it already and can't stop looking at the windows of celestial light. The scene reminds me of gleaming polished teeth, as if piled upon a hill in some strange dream; a beautiful one that inspires a youthful sense of joy. The piazza starts to fill with the day's tourists and I am for a meal and a siesta. A bowl of Arrabbiata satiates the hunger pangs while mouthfuls of cooled water quench my thirst. Sleepy after this, I retire to my room. The blinds flutter ever so gently in the breeze while shafts of light criss-cross the room. I stare at this vision of tranquillity then fall into a deep and restful sleep, only to wake up to the sound of lovebirds on the ledge outside. Soon I'm at the station again and on my journey down south to Lecce.

APRIL 7th

A waft of flowers mingles with heated pavements on some Leccese street. I'm walking along in lighter clothing now and the sallowed complexions of winter begin to pinken in the suncreamed light. A Vespa speeds by and nearly knocks me over. It could be so quick – just like that – then all that consciousness would evaporate. But I survived and do not feel phased. In fact, today I feel elated with the strengthening sun's summer vibe. Strains of 'Summer Breeze' by the Isleys can even be heard on some bar radio followed by 'Happy' which sets the day's mood. My students are upbeat today too and we laugh at nothing or even everything until I trip trop down the school steps to the corner bar for a large spremuta d'arancia. Bless this cooling drink with its tinkly iced cubes taking way the edge of thirst. I'm so happy today that even the man with hardened eyes seems to have a softer edge. The cheese shop sets me straight though. One grumpy tone can have a devastating effect . I reflect how one man's good day's another man's bad. How we seek to cling and grasp at happiness but it can be fleeting when you absorb the weightiness of human emotions around you.

At the flat, my landlord also seems glum. In fact, he's muttering to himself on some injustice. I see no reason to participate and head for a sleep after lunch which sees gleaming scarlatine poms sitting proudly by a wodge of Gorgonzola and even more. A few plump olives complete the scene – as brave as the bold there by a yeasty panino. Famished then satiated, I sleep a sound sleep, not even concerned with the yappings and shoutings; the chattings and slamming. And I sleep on till it's time to return to the school.

They're as loyal as dogs, my favourite class. My adults have that endearing mixture of pride and humility. We laugh. We even sing. It's great and I enjoy it. But the day's been long and so I return to my flat, with its unusual features – the round bath; the triffid mirror and the strange wardrobe. My flat. My home. For now anyway.

APRIL15th

There's the bin lifting man on his way again. I wonder what he's thinking about today. I know what I'm thinking about and it is home. Soon I am at the airport, after the town and the olive groves and the motorway whizz by; after the salmon-pink villa and the posters, the Vespas and trucks; the palms and Oleander; the glimpses of sea. Brindisi. I shall return in a fortnight and will record.

APRIL 25th

The taxi swings open. Three flights and two suitcases later. All Englanded up. Loved up. Eastered up. Chocolate fixed. Like a frozen still. There's the bin man lifting again. The shady one looks across at me. The bank guard's still guarding. The bar's still buzzing. The Vespas are still whizzing. I'm back. The slight rise in temperature sees a little more flora. The cats a wee bit more lazy. The old man on Viale Japigia has beads of sweat on his forehad. He hasn't forgotten to be immaculate though. He's wearing an

ironed shirt and creased trousers. Probably his daughter's efforts. He looks tired; as old

as the hills but yet he has a vibrancy in one eye as if a little bit of him retained his youth.

And what a youth I imagine he had, there on his Vespa with his girlfriends. He would

have been handsome once. Now he has one foot in life, the other for sleep.

Via Oberdan is alway well kept; more so than the adjoining streets. A smart street with

smart shops and smart palazzi.

The shops are lively and voices echo the streets. Noone seems to be out of sorts today.

It's as if a collective consciousness has grabbed at the positive. Even mundane shopping

has taken on a summer hue. The sunglasses have taken residence on my head. I spot one

of my students. We chat a while and I notice, again, that sense of how, in one sense, the

world is the same over. We talk of normal things, though in Italian, of everyday concerns

and wishes. A butterfly floats by. Cafes buzz with locals and tourists alike. The

volume's up and I see that thing I wanted - that sense of warmth and childhood holidays;

the sense of sunlight on the skin and summer perfumed air; the birds singing and palms

swaying.

As evening falls, a different vibe takes hold, but the inevitable advance of summer stays

with me. My classes have the shuttered windows open now. We laugh. I hope they

learn. We chat. We move forward on our road. This thing we share. Life.

APRIL 28th

Glorious days. Everyone has that aura that comes with warmer weather and the shedding

of layers. All is well and so I feel this all Italian summer day will be a happy one. But

then I hear them talk about the old lady. Mugged there in the town centre. Midday. On her way to church. Pushed to the ground she was very shaken and injured. How sad. Her cross was ripped from her neck, they said. And so I remembered there is no room for complacency. The days that are fine don't always correlate with the finest times. And so it was when the young woman walked towards the town and they sprayed her with some noxious substance and robbed her. And so every day unharmed and uninjured is a blessing; too not witness the atrocities another. So, as I stroll along Via Trinchese, I think how random life can be and that timing is sometimes all. Or is it pre-planned this thing called life, with its highs and lows; the goods and the bads. I remember, once, long ago, at university. A mellow mood. Nothing harsh. Sunny I think. Mild. A car appeared with four young men. Reading it was, near London. They opened a door as if to abduct me. Terrified I ran into a shop. A moment that could have gone either way. My guardian angel was there that day so off they sped all criminal and malice. It's those surprises I don't care for in the mellow moments.

But mostly life is mundane or fine.

And this town, with all its happenings is only one of many – across the land, across the world. How can we assume?

The small ones just as much.

The tiny too.

It's not the buildings, you see, or the potted palms ore even the animals strutting around. It's the people. Everywhere. What they say and what they do. And sometimes what they fail to do.

APRIL 30TH

Matera with its Sassi cave dwellings.   These days some of these have been turned into hotels which appeal to anyone who has a propensity for pot-holing. I, however, choose to stay in a normal kind not far from said caves, after my train run, which saw me cross from the Salento to Basilicata then repair for my hotel.

It's pretty cool, Matera, not least because it was used to make 'The passion of Christ' some years ago. However, the thing I liked most about it is that sense of ancient that renders time irrelevant.

When I arrived, I grabbed myself a little brunch before taking in the sights. I was not the only one to be wandering around the ancient place. The first thing that struck me was how different the town is – much as Alberobello and Otranto. Italy fascinates in this way. You'll find each town unique. With their cultural idisoyncrasies as well as dialect, the place is such a draw; along with its obvious charms.

Here I was walking along stone pathways that had been so for centuries. I decided to visit the 'Casa Grotta' to find out how it was for the inhabitants of the town back then. It must, indeed, have been extremely grotty.   In bygone times, people would share their 'home' with their livestock. So, along with Nonna, you would maybe find the odd horse or pig. I must say this was probably preferable to living with a bunch of humans. And as I walked, surrounded by the old stone dwellings, I felt less a sense of claustrophobia and more one of the eternal stretches of time; a thousand stories behind its walls. The hotel gave me quite a view, and when I slept I felt a millennia of life surrounding me and absorbing my bones.

I was fascinated by Matera and felt that it would not be a bad choice for future TEFL experiences. Perhaps I could even take up pot-holing. Never say never.

CHAPTER EIGHT - MAY

MAY 3rd

The early light sees me on my balcony looking out across the rooftop town, mishmashed shades of salmon pink and fawn. The terraced gardens pretty in their rest. Some of the palazzi are quite high. My first - five floors - and this one four. Across the tops, I see another, maybe seven. The pillared concrete reminds me of sadder times.

1982 it was. Heartbroken.

A broken love and far, far worse. I'd fled to London to escape. Depressed and grieving for it all. I stayed in Dalston for a while. London's finest East of end. Hackney. Acne. 'ackney. Agh.

On the 20th floor of a high rise, that I existed for a while. All wilted and forlorn and then the view from my balcony far across the city. Evening lights were magical. Sometimes an early fog would render it all impressionist, with not much discernible but perched there on that jutting balcony, like nails on a blackboard and tripping on some paving stone. Uncomfortable. Smarting. Looking down on boxed in lives or across the token Green.

For me a temporary thing, being a nomad. For some permanence.

I recall the metal lift which stank of urine and the damp and littered floor. It rarely worked and so would come the flights of stairs down broken glass and stains; through unfriendly faces. A street gang once surrounded me. Tired after hours on a train, I stated quite assertively, 'Look. Have a heart. I've just been travelling for hours and want to get home'.

They parted to release me. Respect.

I got it right this time.

And then I recall the seedy ones offering jobs; the market and the thieves.

I soon left all this behind like a giant's knapsack filled with cutting stones. It was put somewhere and abandoned.

My next base had been Clapham Common. More civilized somehow, I'd even acquired a cat. Dodo. Gorgeous thing; so loved. Sadly it eventually lived up to its name.

A slight chill takes hold. I miss that cat so much, yet so long ago. I don't miss Dalston or the lift. The lift once had me squared. Stuck in there for twenty floors with two thugs. I can't bear to recall. They followed me to my flat. A guardian angel saw me right. A light and someone in. They fled. Shudder. This my life. Only just. On a knife edge. I've never trusted lifts since. Whenever I see them, I feel anxious, and so I avoid. My neighbours never understand. I do. That's all that matters.

I once saw a man in central London. Dead, I think. I and the others scurried on. Stabbed, I believe. Right near the best and busy shops. The city streets were thronged. The police surrounded him like angels. An ambulance nearby. Carry on. We all did. We all do.

I watch the early risers leave their homes. Home. An interesting thought. What defines a home?

This isn't home for me. It's home for some who might have been here since year dot; their first steps and their second. Perhaps they got their hearts broken too and pass him on the street. Mended by time and age. Maybe they are incomers, like me. The old girl crossing near the car is not. She's been here almost a century. She's talking to a younger man; her son most probably. The street lights snaffle out for the new hours. So when I see a small black and white cat walking on a jutting balcony and smelling plants, I think of Dodo, my beloved feline friend. We'd sleep all spoons. He'd even groom me. The final time I saw him, he was in my arms and gave me such a look. A meld of love and sorrow.

I think he knew. Cats do.

I wonder if he knows, somehow, just how much I loved him. I still do.

One of the palazzo walls is mustard yellow. I don't normally like this shade, but backdropped with a pale celestial sky and the Bougainvilla, it looks a picture. It take one in fact. A lady notices from her balcony and stares then returns inside laden with washing.

It's 7 am and I'm ready. A steady day ensues.

MAY 6th

I have some good news and it's of the most mundane type. Finally I can dry my clothes on the balcony and I can't express how helpful this is. I'm becoming the keenest clothes washer in town as I dangle the things from several silk scarves tied together across the balcony. I don't even need to worry about drips, as they dry quickly now with the smell of sun drenched heat.

So, I have a new routine. As I siesta, my clothes are prepared and can even be worn in time for school at 4.

I feel more spruce and have less need of the lovely laundry ladies, though I still pop in to see the whirring and whooshing; the spinning and ironing from the ancient machines and giant presses, and the tissued paper packages of clothes as end result.

MAY 7th

The warmth is tangible now and sun dappled streets strewn with petals line my walks through Lecce. Today, though, I'm heading for Torre dell'Orso with my friend Maria. As we take the scenic route, along olive groved plots, with plump birds caw cawing from rooftops, a sense of summer smiled on us. The approach to the beach saw that others had the same idea but it was suitably early to avoid whole swathes of beachgoers. Not quite sunbathing weather, but certainly for a stroll. So we walk along the sand and take photos with our phones, enjoying the ambience and the gentle sea breezes. Thoughts of childhood come back to me. Of sand dunes stretching to wide golden beaches on hot July days way back. Perhaps 1970. Ireland it was, the west coast. Beautiful. I recall the sensation of running up and down dune, with small patches of gorse sprinkled here and there; the delicious aroma of the sea. And then childhood pleasures swimming in the shallows, a lilo afloat or pottering by some rock pool to admire the fascinating contents therein; a shy crab, some shrimps and even a starfish. And then the pleasure of watching awhile before a picnic, our sandy hands the only fly in the ointment. So coming back to 2013 the beach lays its wares before us. A tempting coastline has attracted some small private boats. A dog runs enthusiastically hither and thither, nimbly climbing the rocks at the end. We soon head for a bar to enjoy a cappuccino. Thus refreshed, we return to the beach and sit awhile on a large towel looking out to sea.

And then I recall the beach on Arran. Cantering atop a pony I could barely ride, aged perhaps 9, towards a forest hill, complete with picknickers. That beast helped himself to a sandwich. The moment struck me powerfully and punctuated a happy time.

Dim and distant memories come now of the Whistling Sands in Wales. Some beach walk as a small child then being carried up a steep rocky hill as the tide came in. The sea seemed wild and frothy below. All memories.

Here the sky is clearest blue today and the sun's warmth makes us sleepy, so for a short while we snooze right there on the beach. Lovely.

However, the weather starts to change and dark, leaden clouds loom over the scene cruelly spurning the new warmth.

We get up and head for the bar to eat a panino. The cheese oozes from the sides, married to a slice of greasy Salami. It hits a spot. I'm hungry. As pregnant clouds release their drops, we head for the car and take a subdued drive back to Lecce. The busy town is scurrying from street to shop and beyond, far away from the beach tranquillity. I return to my flat and sleep a while. The day has tired me, though in the best possible way.

I don't know what I dreamt about but I like to think it was of golden sand dunes on a hot summer's day, way back in time.

MAY 10th

There's a hue to the skies today that tells of simple joys and pleasant dreams. The pale blues warmed by the rays ensures an upbeat sense of forwardness. All feels positive and right.

The day begins in a small corner of the Patisseria, consuming one fat and floury cornetto. This is hardly a criticism, but more a point of fact. The jammy centre gloops a little onto my fingers and so a delicate wipe of the serviette suffices embarrassment avoidance.

A gentleman of about 40 peers over his morning paper and scrutinizes through expensive looking eyeware. A slightly disapproving glance soon reminds me so. With jammy gloop safely recovered and lips wiped clean of any sticky residue, I feel I am woman enough to pursue my day.

The school today is looking bright and has the perfumed smell of summer, in part because the secretary has placed glorious blooms in vases on her desk and partly because all seem to be wearing summer perfumes.

My students look a little weary as exam time approaches. I know how important it is to them and feel an empathy that I try to express in the gentleness of my voice and manner. Furrowed brows perplex over adverbial clauses and phrasal verbs. Who am I to blame them for all is confusing and subjective?

We practice many times the same things and like a coin that finally slots into a machine, some are there, whilst others flail behind. Enough is enough for this day and so the lessons end and onto the street scene.

A naughty nip into the delicatessen sees me eyeing up their ware. Earthenware pots of scrumptious foods all laid out in neat containers. I see huge olives and seafood married to peppers and parsley. A swidge of lemon here; a dash of balsamic there. It is divine. I stole away with the goods, a guilty sense that the rest of the world can't share this feast. The queue is always there and it doesn't surprise! Then I nip into the launderette to tell the ladies I have some stuff for them. No matter how the presses and oppressive heat hammer them; the demands of endless finery to sort, they are always kind and pleasant. They regard me, I think, as a younger person but I am not about to complain. Then into the tea shop. The only difference is that here it is regarded as medicinal rather than a daily pleasure. So on asking for one, the lady enquires as to my ailment. As far as I know, I don't have one, and if I do it's entirely unrelated to the tea.

The supermercato is busy as always at this time. Like predictive text, they think they know what I want and can be premature with their offerings. I'm a changeable one sometimes and can fancy the other. But I like their guesses and their simpatia. It helps my day along.

Waiting for the vegetables is, however, an entirely other matter. Here le verdura are a very important part of any meal and you will see nonna and bisnonna; mama and daughter queuing for their turn. Not here the pre-packed variety but a slightly harrassed looking man who serves each and every customer according to demands. Sometimes these are protracted as each and every vegetable is scrutinized by the buyer or rejected in favour of the plumper one.

You need to save a nice swodge of time in this pursuit and I recommend a quick nip in first thing before the ladies arrive en masse.

You must not lift nor poke nor hold as this is not the done thing here. You must look from a respectful distance, and only touch if for the till.

You will wait as the cashier chats to Signora, if you please, and this could also take some time. The more you are part of the fabric of the place, the more you are accepted and embraced.

The bread man waves and smiles. He jokes about today's special panino; a Semolina special. He holds it up and waves it about. We laugh. I shake my head. Not today Josephine.

Right outside the door sits a man, cross-legged and begging. He looks up at me imploringly. I am, by nature, a very sympathetic type and give him a few Euros. He has a walking stick to one side and looks dirty and unkempt. I've seen the same man looking a whole lot better, even running down the road! I say nothing. If he feels the need to do this, who am I to judge? Italy is expensive at times.

MAY 17th

I wake to a peachy dawn and decide to have a little room run. It's 4.30 am but I've slept well and the birds are singing outside. What more reason do you need?

The shower feels especially good after this, and I'm really happy as I'm going on a road trip with my student Ana Rosa back along the coast.

The grand Patisseria is the place to start and so it is that I consume with relish a large cappuccino and even larger cornetto. It suddenly strikes me that I would never eat so many of these for breakfast in England, but somehow here it makes sense and is a fine and healthy thing to do. How I love such delusional trifles!

Ana Rosa is prompt and swigs an Espresso before we set off on our long journey. The whole experience of being a car passenger in Italy excites me. This, perhaps counter intuitive as we know how the driving can be. However to sit and watch the world flash by and see that world with virgin eyes, then to drink in every inch of difference and colour and shade and hue. It's a wonder. The pastel buildings sit pert in barren fields by road signs and racing cars. A palm tree here and there reminds where we are and the olive groves surround some whitewashed villa.

It's a hot and sticky day so I am so glad I remembered to buy water. Firstly we head to Gallipoli. I've been here before, but not with company so this is nice. A large wicked looking ice-cream takes on hilarious colour as it gloops unashamedly onto the cafe floor. You know how it is here !

I am thoroughly ashamed but Ana Rosa laughs and laughs until I can barely contain myself.   Interjected with our stroll are snippets of her life and mine; some surprises and revelations. The golden light buoys us on towards the harbour and we pass the fishermen mending nets. Taking photos here and there, we stop for lunch at the one. The one I've eaten at before by the sea with the view. Spaghetti alla vongole. I slurp each oily strand with gusto for it is truly delicious and so are the views of sea and sand and pastel buildings.

Before long we stroll back to the car, laughing at almost everything. She is very funny and so am I. The drive past the sea, sees Ana reflecting on the sea's tone. It is green. Yes, green and limpid. I feel I am watching a holiday programme but I am here as we whizz past pine forests and glimpses of sea and more pine to more sea to long drivey roads past whizzy cars. Being in the mood, we decide to head even further south, right down to Santa Maria de Leuca. This the most southerly part of the heel, where it's said that a rock formation there resembles a sleeping dragon. We see the little church where once there lay an ancient temple built for Minerva.

Small yellow flowers sprinkle the ground before and around and we stand awhile and talk of Greece. It's over there and Ana has been many times in a boat. Not a ferry but a small boat with   friends. It takes a long time but it's worth it she says. I can believe it. It's very quiet here. Perhaps the time of day. Siesta. Many of the villas are the holiday homes of rich Milanese so there is an emptiness to the place, an isolated outpost feel. I glance out to sea and see nothing but sea and more sea and the ivory light.

And so it is that we climb back into her small green car and drive up the Mediterranean coast, past cliffs, and rocks, along winding roads. The landscape is very different here.

No beaches, just rock that plunges into bluest seas and a high winding road that meanders and twist with alacrity. The whole coastline contains fascinating grottoes such as the Zinsulusa and rocks that the brave, or foolish, depending on your point of view, like to dive from.

Heading along the Adriatic, you eventually come to Capo d'Otranto and this leads you on to the small town of Castro, Trojan's place. Ana buys some nuts and we sit awhile looking out to sea. And then the hill of snakes. It doesn't entice but has magnificent views of where the Turks once invaded. Little watchtowers dot the coast and poppies sprinkle the roadside. The winding roads go up and down, all rollercoaster mashed with summer. The brightness of the day lifted our spirits for we were both a little weary from the past few days and our chat wandered from past to present. There is nothing like a car journey for airing the deepest recesses of our mind. The eyes focus on the road, the head focused on the soul. In fact we had some similarities that surprised me but we also shared a sadness that crossed all cultures.

The craggy mountain crops and dark blue sea seemed to support all this soul searching and we found solace, not only in each others' company, but also in the southern air. Seven months into the experience, I wondered how it would be to live in Lecce permanently, though I knew in my heart of hearts that I wouldn't want to, for several reasons. Partly because of emotional ties back home, but also because Lecce, from this outside perspective, seems like a closed if beautiful jewel; the sense of the landlocked pervasive. It was easier to see, from a distance, the lack of water and the heaviness of too many buildings. You know you are missing something and that something is space and nature and sea.

So back in Lecce, I feel a sense of claustrophobia as the buildings engulf and the noise levels rise. We are back in the town and it's dusk fall.

Perhaps Lecce is not the answer. I think I knew it never was.

MAY 18th

There is something about this time of year that makes me smile. It's not just the obvious summer vibe, but also the way life is suddenly lived. Gone are the dark days before Christmas and the furrowed brows. Bring in the sweaty palm and Armani wafts.

The day begins with simple shower and then I trip trop down the stairs. Today I'm for a Spremuta so I sip on the sweet sticky juice and refreshed emerge all butterfly onto the street. The only fly in the ointment today, the traffic fumes, rising in the breeze.

And then I see him -the mysterious man sitting in his car, still looking across to a palazzo. The sinister presence is accompanied this time by another equally sinister. What do they want, I wonder? I can't imagine why they sit and wait so long. The engine's always off and they do nothing. They sit and they stare, and don't avert their eyes. I do believe, they're waiting for someone to emerge. And then I see it. A man appears through the portone, with briefcase in hand, and they kerb crawl him from a distance. The man is oblivious to this indignity and seems relaxed. I have no idea what it's about, and perhaps it's best I don't.

I'm meeting up with Maria today in Piazza del Duomo. And so I walk happily, amongst the summer dwellers and the street vendors, practically swinging my bag. The light's intoxicating and I feel a light feathery thing floating along. It helps that I'm wearing sensible shoes today.

When I reach the Piazza Oronzo, I see the crowds of teenagers outside McDonald's and the tourists in Alvino's, so all seems as it should. The taxi drivers wave now, as they recognize me as I pass.

Belonging. Hardly, but it almost passes for it. I'm an old hand now. I pass a street vendor selling sunglasses and almost tempted, pause a moment. He looks imploringly at me and I concede. I don't need them as I'm wearing some, but this seems unimportant. I see the sleepy dog outside his shop and round into the piazza. Beautiful. Always. And then, early, I enter the Duomo to spend five minutes communing with all that is holy. A calming sense of peace pervades the air, and I look with fresh eyes at the gilded and the painted artwork therein and sit a while and pray. I pray for peace and sanctuary; the things most precious to me.

And outside again, into intense sunlight, there's the man sculpting by the wall. I watch a while and marvel at his work. He is modest and carries on.

Entering the bar, there sits Maria, looking lovely in the corner and waiting for me. She's happy as she's grasped the Simple Past and wants to tell me so. We do a mini lesson there and then. She's cracked it. That feels good. And so we amuse each other by talking in the past. It is very funny when it comes to ordering drinks. And so I say to my dear friend, 'I really wanted a Spremuta this morning' and she goes and gets me one. It's a great vat of the stuff all squidged and squeezed and tangy but nothing a naughty mouthful of sugar won't cure.

And then for the tempting treats the assistant gives us as a gesture of courtesy, for we are loyal customers. A Zeppola consumed.

We chat a while, mostly of our families but also of the Simple Past and I tell her of my day so far and how I entered the Duomo and saw the gilded and the painted and the beauty of the place.

She smiles.

She asks me how I'm finding Lecce, and I give an honest reply. Mixed. I like some things and not others. She looks offended and I wish I could retract. I explain it's more an internal than external thing and how lovely I have found my students; not only my students but also the people I encounter day to day.

But there was a life once before you see, another life.

Other places and other people.

It changes one's perspectives.

And so, much like visiting the same place twice, it doesn't strike quite as it should.

A poem I once wrote:

'He never ventured far from then,

Yet always wanted more than now,

Weakened by his own existence,

Affected only by the sane.'

There was once the world of 'It should have been me' and 'Never can say goodbye'; the Clangers and the Clackers; the Vesta meals and milkshakes; The Saint and Man about the House. There was all this stuff and that was just a fraction of a whole. Dallas and Dynasty; Bologna; Siena; Viareggio; University; marriage; children. So many things potted into a life.

Sad that as you get older the gloss falls from our eyes and we see things as they are , in all their mundanity . Sad to lose those rose tinted ones that render each new experience completely magical.

I think she understands. I hope so.

MAY 25th

The hayfever is pretty bad and not something I'm used to. I surmise the pollen's different here and so I cough and sneeze and wheeze and splutter through the day. But that is not the worst of it. It makes me sleepy and not of this world; disengaged, detached. Uncomfortable. I head for the Farmacia on Via Oberdan, where the efficient assistant shows me her wares. I choose one and hope for the best. A few days in finds some relief but not complete and so I struggle on, as you do. It's worse at night, as if someone has wodged an entire box of tissue up each sorry nostril so I try steam but mostly I suffer.

I heard that someone got shot some hours ago on a beach somewhere. It makes me shudder. Probably gang related. There is always a grey to go with the gold.

The heat's intense as I walk towards Dok. I smile and wave at the posh veg shop as I pass and spotting Signora Rizzi at her chats, head a different way. She sees me but the distance requires only a wave.

As I pass the bookshop and all the tourist guides; I see one on Bologna.

I did some private lessons there once. And what an odd bunch too! One Sicilian spoke of women running naked on a beach whilst I tried to teach him Question tags. Disconcerting and strange. Another showed me photos of his goats, while I attempted conversation lessons. All this, whilst my mother-in-law pottered the apartment and scrubbed the floor.

Those were the days when I'd return to England to enjoy a Sunday breakfast of Bacon and Eggs. It seems so strange now, but then so normal or perhaps I'd watch Dallas or Dynasty. The '80s. What a decade! It started with a broken heart and ended in Barletta, strolling the beaches of the Gargano. Somewhere in the middle came a brief stint in Athens too. So hot! Having survived being stalked by a pack of wild dogs in the suburbs, late one night by dog whispering, I recall the flight home and the crazy passenger who toyed with the emergency exit. Combined with the turbulence and the pacing Greeks, it's not an experience I care to repeat. The'80s. Lycra. I remember going to those exercise classes then watching 'Bread'. The clothes. Appalling. Awful. Great baggy monstrosities or shoulder pads and the birth of the Mullet. But 1989 saw me flying to Puglia where that light and those palms did away with all that. Margaret Thatcher and her poll tax outrage. I wasn't there at the time. London was by now a bad memory. I was in a different place completely. And then came Reading, the town. A late university degree. Italian of course. Whiteknights campus. Neat. I had a blue bicycle. Loved it. Loved my lectures and my seminars. Loved my studies and my course. Learnt a bit of German. Loved the book shop and the library. Love. Love Love. Listened to my favourite sounds on a Walkman and learnt a lot.

Home visits. More Bacon and Eggs; Dallas and Bread. Then came Viareggio, a treasure in itself. As summer month spent studying in Tuscany. Perfect it was. I often think of it and how perfect it was. Suzanne Vega playing, though I felt neither small nor blue; just pink and bright. Sparkly it was . Light and fresh. Good times.

CHAPTER NINE – JUNE

JUNE 1st

It's been a while, perhaps some twenty-five long years since I went to the grand old city

of Bari. Of course, I don't include the many airport pass-throughs en route to other parts.

I'm going with the other teachers so we set off bright and early on a Freccia Bianca in

these final days in Italy. They've never been before.

We chat about our time and compare experiences. I tell them of my past; the days in

Puglia long ago.

And then we arrive.

From the station we head through bustle streets towards the old town.. Notorious

historically for petty crime, given its labyrinth of alleyways, this is also the best part.

The old town. The real stuff. We feel quite safe as there are plenty of folk about and no

sense of the little mice, i topi, today. Finding a pizzeria to lunch in after our amblings, I

drink a sweet, sticky Limonata. The natural sugars buoy our energies and I'm reminded

of the topi I experienced two years ago in Barletta with husband James. Approached we

were, then cornered down some blind alley. These kids on mopeds looked quite

intimidating but when they found out we were English from near Manchester, a childish

innocence overcame their demeanour. Why? Because they loved Man. United they said.

And off they sped leaving two surprised people shaken but not stirred.

We did the tourist trail today. Bari cathedral and the Petruzzelli theatre, then sat near the

sea and daydreamed about the yachts bobbing ostentatiously before us. A strong

reminder of wealth and privilege. The expensive seafarers there, laid bare yet powerful.

We head to the modern quarter Borgo Murattiano, after this to look at some shops. The criss-crossed streets of the new town, a workaday world constructed under Joachim Morat way back in early 19th century - is a very different ambience;one of industry and speed.

The people hurry and scurry as in any big city. We prefer the old ways; the lazy lilt of the water lapping against some millionaire's yacht.

Soon it's time for our return, so laden with spoils, we head to the station, past 'those to be wary of' and 'those to pity'onto La Freccia Bianca, and back to Lecce we whizz.

We're tired now. All experienced up. Months of it. Months of work and play.

Lecce seems more tranquil in comparison. Bari, with its economic drive and gatherings of people is for another time - probably for the airport or for passing through, in my case. I respect Bari, but it's not for me.

Back in my flat, I lie back in a bath and reflect on the day – the alleys of the old town and the shops in the new. It all sends me to a peaceful place and I soon fall asleep in my Leccese bed.

JUNE 3rd

My husband's arriving today, although it will be fleeting, and so I spend my day in sweet anticipation till the evening. I've booked us into a central hotel, near all the sights. The day seems to drag but then, all tasks complete, I hop into a taxi with a small bag and make my way to the hotel. I've very tired these days. Eight months have taken their toll and as I lie in my luxury bed, I'm struggling to stay awake. It's very late when he arrives. A call from reception notifies me of my other half. And in he comes. Embrace. He's excited by the visit and the charm of the place. We don't sleep till late then have a hotel breakfast of cakes and sweetmeats by the burbling of a coffee machine. We laugh and share, as you do and I leave him to explore the town as I head for my lessons that morn.

The evening's exquisite for after class, instead the lonesome trek across six lanes and the jagged paving stones beneath two weary feet, I'm met by James who holds my hand back to the flat and once inside runs me a bath and sets about cooking dinner. He's all at home here and loves the place. So, as I soak in scented bath, I smell homely wafts of garlic and pomodori from the busy kitchen stove. My meal is delicious and made with love. We dessert in gelato, a little wine. And so a new perspective on the town. Lecce a deux, though soon to be adieu.

JUNE 4th

More exams at the school. Nerves and stress are palpable and remind me of my '70s school days. There were two dreads back then: the results and injections, which were an unpleasant reality of the times. The former saw us victim to norm referencing. I remember the teacher entering the classroom with a pile of exam scripts, all marked with the red pen, and the ensuing anxiety. A fear. At the front and top would be the circled mark but beside the position in class so our class of 31 would sit in absolute terror as each result was read out from top to bottom, names and all. The girls would have to go out to the front and take their script, all eyes upon them. Invariably the same people at both ends, every time. The teacher's tone would change half way through to one of disapproval so all the girls in the bottom half would face their humiliations perhaps nine times in a week. It was enough to make you despise the system.

The latter saw us lined up, along the corridor, having been told some tall tale of the agony by those who'd gone before. And when you finally arrived at the medical room, the smell of antiseptic and the sight of large needles in a bowl, was enough to turn you funny. And yes it pricked back, then, unlike now.

But afterwards, the joy and pure relief. Done and over till the next time. Often not long before Christmas too.

And so I look at my pupils with real empathy. Although they don't face the teacher's ire, or the public humiliations of the norm reference, still they are nervous and stressed as these exams are important to them. Only a few are there for mere fun. Many are doing it for work purposes.

I'm not there when they do their exams, as externals examiners are brought in and so I decide to go to the seaside with my husband. We take the bus to San Cataldo, sitting like two warmed buns on a stove. When we arrive, it's very quiet as most people are at work and so we have the scene to ourselves. We sit upon a wall and look out to sea, admiring the glittering waterborne lights. James decides to take a dip though I don't. Instead I find a quiet spot and read awhile, whilst looking out to sea for the in between moments. I've nearly finished my time here, and my overwhelming sense is one of tiredness. It's a beautiful country, but I feel a little weary now; perhaps ready for a bit of rain and wind. I cuddle the thought to myself – autumn days all wrapped up against some northern wind; with gloves and hat all rosy cheeked, in England.

The grass always greener.

I realise at that moment how much I miss the autumn golds and russets and the fallen; the constant rain and leaden skies. Perhaps this, seems odd to some, but I'm from the north. It's in my blood.

We have a drink in a small bar, with its reserved locals eyeing us then later head to lunch in a small rustic trattoria. For me it's a simple Spaghetti alla Marinara and for James the Carbonara. There are no frills in this place, but the food's exquisite. We finish off with Gelato and an Espresso shot.

Returning to Lecce, the town seems busy in comparison and we retire for a siesta.

Later that day in school, I see my pupils. They are a bag of nerves. Some have finished others not and so I try to be gentle as I teach and support them in their revisions.

Looking through the window onto small side streets, I think about the morning spent by the sea. How lovely, I reflect, to see the twinklings and the lappings of tiny waves on the shore; to sit awhile in the sun, half dozing by a wall then eat simple food in a small trattoria. How perfect it was to have those moments away from the bustle and stress.

I reflect on how I love the sea. I'd dearly like to live by it and watch its changing moods. I imagine a stormy Atlantic coast with crashing waves and jagged cliffs, a cottage there atop: I'd look out in the evenings and at dawn, warmed cocoa in hand and drink it all in. Lovely.

JUNE 5th

As each lesson passes I say goodbye to my students. Each lesson, I take in their laughter and expressions, to gather for my memories and a few photos too. I can conclude that these are amongst the best people I have ever met - not only warm and kind, but utterly hilarious. Their humour knows no bounds. And so it's goodbye to the little ones, though

I don't press the point and it's goodbye to the big ones in all their glory. It's goodbye to the school and the other teachers. It's also goodbye to the two fat pigeons who sat together opposite my classroom. I look around the classroom walls, still sporting posters from the kids and close the door shut tight.

My husband is waiting for me by the school and so we walk, hand in hand, along the roads until we reach the daily challenge of the six-laned one. Perhaps it is because he climbs and has the skills of balance; but he navigates his way across, a real pro from the start. We trip along the uneven criss-crossed paving stones and both wave to the bank guard. He smiles amused at this new routine. Then we turn towards the shops, past the Celtic shop where nothing ever happens and the ancient tobacconists. We buy some food and then repair to the flat, both tired, James from long travels and me from a long time here.

Tired of Lecce. Perhaps. A little. It's not so simple though. I adore my students and their winning ways, but perhaps the beauty of the town has not quite taken me, as it should. And yet it is a brilliant place, and I could list its virtues. Not even its vices are the reason. It's all to do with time. There is a time for everything, and perhaps I would have felt differently some twenty years ago. It's also to do with water, and the lack of. And finally, just to do with age. Those who I might have spent time with all those years ago are now married and busy. There is little time for frivolities. I am the same. I do not care for late nights, because I no longer can nor wish to. I am a quiet animal these days. And so the Disco days are gone and all the evenings partying; the sociable nights and the streams of friends. Gone. Because we change. I've changed.

My life is now a mosaic of all that I am and all that I was. The pieces fit but some fell off, on the journey.

And so I watch, a little wearily, the youngsters zooming round the town, on moped or the girls dressed up for big nights out. I understand, but it tires me.

I love the space that peaceful brings where, no sound, can break your thoughts.

I love the days when nothing rings and no one knocks at the door. I like to snooze, with jazz playing softly in the background, and gone are the days of Rock and all that alternative stuff.

They're gone, and some have passed.

My husband is like me, and craves a quietened room. How boring this would once have seemed, in distant youth and past.

My first time back in Italy after 1974, was to Bologna in 1986. April it was. Beautiful sunshine fell on Piazza Maggiore's tower. Beautiful it was. All budding interest in life. Like spring, all fresh and new with anticipation.

And I recall walking through the porticoes and marvelling at their difference, all visually aesthetic and delight.

Every morsel eaten was divine, all vibrant and exciting. Youth.

It was of course just that – my age and not the place. And so if I'd come to Lecce back in 1986, perhaps I'd have felt that buzz of life whilst walking through the town or stayed out a little later to see the dawn, not like now with my woolly hat in winter as I catch a nap and doze at slatted blinds.

My husband is waiting for me, and that feels right.

JUNE 8th

In two days time I'll be a travelling back to England, but my husband leaves today. I peep out from my balcony and then across my room. A large packing job lies ahead with all the moving and leavings to come. Only a couple more crosses of the six lanes. Hope I survive them!

He's still here and so the sorrow that might have been has become a bridge to the future. Our future. It makes now seem ephemeral. And that it is. I return these days to a meal cooked with loving hands. My husband's. I can share my day with him. And we laugh. How we laugh. He likes it here. Of course he likes the cafe on the corner with its sweetmeats a nd the golden light of Via Umberto. He likes the old centre and the Duomo. He likes the cafes and the market; the food and the climate. He likes Davide the newsagent and Maria my friend. And so we sit, like two fluff pigeon looking out across the way and point and chat, relating to it all through fresh and ancient eyes. We remark on the garden and the terraces all planty pot and cat. We observe the returners and the leavers as we sit and drink large cups of tea as if preparing for the return. So by the afternoon, with James all packed and ready, it is a little sad to wave goodbye again and watch him speed off in his taxi.

JUNE 9th

My final day's spent packing. Feverishly. Of course it got postponed. Foolishly perhaps. Trying to wodge it all in one large case. And then the time of reckoning, when things are binned or left for future tenants. Why take the duvet back with me, the one that cost an arm and leg?And so I spend my day, one foot already on the plane. I've said goodbye to those I know and hugged and exchanged addresses. I've said goodbye to the posh veg shop couple; Davide and the corner bar. I've said goodbye to the landlord and his wife and the two fat cats down the street. I've waved goodbye to the bank guard though he doesn't know it. I've seen Harb for the last time and not seen Bin lifter. Neither have I seen Signora Rizzi, though I can't say I'm lamenting. And so I take my large case the few streets to the President. I've given the flat back to the landlord and this will be my final night. I lie in the bath that evening, reflecting on my eight months here. An airport taxi's ordered for the morn. Isolation, loneliness, perhaps a little down. I've lived here for eight months like a sad butterfly, with no fresh meadow to explore. I'm all Lecced up and moving on from this beautiful place. This strange, successful town with its claustrophobic air; its golden Baroque centre; sleepy cats and yappy dogs; Bin lifter and Harb; Signoral Rizzi; the posh veg shop couple; Davide; Ernesto the ancient admirer; my students much loved; the nice stationer's; the corner sweetmeat bar; the mysterious car sitter. All of it is coming to an end; even the birds that wake me every morning and the scorpion that lurks behind the cooker; the street vendors, beggars and the strange piazza folk. And Dok and Dok's beggar. In a waiting room. All closing now. All done. All. I've spent eight months in Lecce now. Spent.

And with the end complete,

I almost ran,

And didn't look behind,

Because I can.

26053683R00122

Printed in Poland
by Amazon Fulfillment
Poland Sp. z o.o., Wrocław